Candace L. Long

Letters To Aleeyah

A Personal Journey Of Generational Healing

ISBN 978-0-9788322-6-1
For Worldwide Distribution
Printed in the U.S.A.

auDEO Publications
A Division of auDEO Media Group, LLC
885 Woodstock Road | Suite 430 – 337 | Roswell, GA 30075-8212
1-866-308-4850
info@CreativityTrainingInstitute.com

TABLE OF CONTENTS

Introduction

Appendix

DEDICATION

I dedicate this book to my forefathers
who served God in Liberty County, Georgia.

Samuel Spry Law
(1775 - 1837)

He started his life as a man of the world and ended it as a devout minister of the Sunbury Baptist Church, dedicated to saving the souls of the plantation slaves.

Josiah Spry Law
(1808 - 1853)

Josiah became a minister and walked in the footsteps of his father, Samuel Law, for he likewise felt deeply the spiritual needs of the people of color.

ACKNOWLEDGEMENTS

There are many whose contributions made this book possible.

First and foremost, I give thanks to Holy Spirit who provided revelation, counsel and direction throughout the research and writing of the book. He never ceases to amaze me with how creative He is in giving wisdom and understanding when I needed it. He is a Wonderful Counselor!

I thank the Lord for three spiritual mentors and "mothers in the faith" whose contributions are immeasurable: Elizabeth Hairston-McBurrows, Sandy Mathis and Barbara Wentroble. I am humbled by your belief in me and inspired by the level of integrity with which you serve the Lord.

I want to acknowledge my sisters of color who faithfully read my early draft and courageously counseled and advised me along the way: Charleyne Davis, Lane Holland, Isabelle Jones, Cynthia Newborne, Gayle Rogers and Mamie Harris Smith. Through you, I learned about the suffering you have had to endure. Thank you for keeping me true to the path God desired for this book.

To D'Ann and Jim Medlin, June Jones and Patsy Carol Logue: thank you for your faithful prayers and encouragement.

I am grateful to the readers of my "levitical monographs" who often wrote to encourage me to keep writing.

And finally, to Aleeyah: thank you for trusting me with your heart.

"Candace Long is an instrument of healing in the Kingdom of God! She fearlessly steps into every painful place of division with the healing power of the Holy Spirit. She is willing to be transparent in dealing with tough issues.

I applaud Candace for the courage and humility she expresses in this book. May the Lord use it to heal the brokenness in His wonderful people, no matter the color or ethnicity!

– Barbara Wentroble –
President & Founding Apostle, International Breakthrough Ministries
CEO, Business Owners For Christ International
Dallas, Texas

Author:
Prophetic Intercession; Praying With Authority; Rise To Your Destiny, Woman of God;
Removing The Veil of Deception; Fighting For Your Prophetic Promises

"Candace Long has done it again. In the pages of this book are the keys to setting people free. I have been a deliverance minister for over 30 years and know that the sexual and emotional abuse in families of all races are in epidemic proportions. Our women need to be healed. ***Letters to Aleeyah*** is a must-read for every woman, regardless of race!

– Sandy Mathis –
Founding Apostle, Sandy Mathis Ministries
Pastor, House of Refuge
Roswell, Georgia

" I believe the Lord gave you this book to open up the windows of heaven over His people of color. In Aleeyah, God has shown you the African American woman, and you articulate beautifully where she fits and her true position in the Lord. We talk about reconciliation between the races, but we have struggled with, *'What does that look like? What does that mean?'* We can't reconcile ourselves, so it's going to take a strong white person to come alongside and say, *'Okay, we want to get it right now!'* You have taken a giant step.

– Gayle Rogers, Ph.D. –
Founder & President, Forever Free, Inc.
President & Founding Apostle, Apostolic Coaching For Empowerment
San Jose, California

Author:
Healing The Traumatized Soul; Offense vs. Woundedness - Bridging Broken Relationships, Presence of God, Vol. I; Intimacy In His Presence, Vol. II

" I was sharing with a pastor friend how you recently addressed the women of color at our last gathering. The pastor could not believe that a white woman would confess the strength that we possess. You are on time for this next generation. Cry loud...somebody needs to hear the voice of the prophet!

– Apostle Dr. Mamie Harris Smith –
Pastor, New Generation Christian Fellowship
Griffin, Georgia

Author:
Detour To Destiny

66 Words cannot express my gratitude to you for writing this book. This topic of generational cleansing and healing has been ignored far too long. My husband and I and our teenage children had a bible study surrounding the biblical truths outlined here and were fascinated and enlightened by what we read. We felt like many questions about our people were answered.

Bless you for having the courage and obedience to do what God said to do. *Letters To Aleeyah* will be on the reading list for our middle and high school students. My kids were absolutely fascinated. It made the Bible come to life for them!

– Isabelle B. Jones, Ed.S. –
Founder & CEO, Masada, Inc.
Gwinnett County, Georgia

66 When you shared that one of your ancestors gave up a prestigious job to minister to slaves, I saw the redemptive stream now flowing through you. You're walking alongside Aleeyah and saying, *'I will not sit on the sidelines and watch my sisters of color suffer. I'm willing to step out in ridicule, and perhaps in judgment, but I cannot be silent on the future God has for my sisters.'*

Your love and compassion for Aleeyah truly comes from the heart of God. I believe the Lord is using you to tear down that dividing wall between blacks and whites and will use *Letters To Aleeyah* to further the cause of racial reconciliation.

– Apostle Cynthia Newborne –
Co-Founder & Pastor, Covenant of Peace Ministries
Woodstock, Georgia

FOREWORD

Throughout the centuries, slavery has been articulated in many ways, yielding economic growth and empires for some, while at the same time leaving nations of people destitute and fearful. They hoped their blatant cries would be heard to bring deliverance, but the cries were all-too-often silenced through persecution, torment and often death.

However, in the midst of their fears, there was a Moses, a deliverer...and a Harriet Tubman, as a Moses...but now there is Aleeyah who dared to cry out, though in a dream. She made a "Macedonian Call" to a 21st century prophet, Candace Long, who stepped beyond her comfort zone to answer the call, "Come and help us!"

The pages of this prophetic book will allow you to join a company of deliverers who will bring many out of bondage, beginning with page 1 of this poignant book.

"And by a prophet the Lord brought Israel out of Egypt."
Hosea 12:13a

– Elizabeth Hairston-McBurrows, Ph.D. –
Founding Apostle, Women With A Call International
Founding Apostle, The Apostolic-Prophetic Connection
Rio Rancho, New Mexico

Author:
The Wonder of Worship, Apostolic Intervention

INTRODUCTION

Whenever I sense the Lord is leading me to write a book, I take a good look at the folder of notes and insights that have accumulated over the months, even years, that the topic has been gestating.

Several years ago, I more fully understood that my specific calling is as a writer… and my "creative children" are framed on the mantelpiece of my heart. Such is the case with *Letters To Aleeyah*. The woman for whom the book is written has been a focal point of much of my research over the last two years. She came to me in a dream…and to be honest, I haven't been able to shake her. I tried to go on with my life, and yet her plea remained an ever-present echo. As a composer, I am very sensitive to sound, and have learned that He often speaks through those who inhabit prophetic dreams…especially someone like Aleeyah.

I have been writing professionally for over 40 years: songs, plays, screenplays, marketing materials, books and more recently, monographs *(i.e., short articles)*. Most of these projects I would describe as "divine assignments," part of my calling as a writer. Interestingly, many of them have involved or specifically addressed needs I have observed in my sisters of color.

Though others may find this book helpful or enlightening, *Letters To Aleeyah* is dedicated to my sisters of color who verbalize their struggle with issues that appear to block them and their children from being fully set free. Lest I be misperceived, I hope you will hear my heart when I say how often I tried to put aside this assignment, fearing I might be viewed as presumptuous.

Inspired By A Dream

Letters To Aleeyah was inspired by a prophetic dream in which I heard the plea of a woman I named Aleeyah – a dream that captured my heart. The Lord reminded me that the Apostle Paul had a similar dream about a man from Macedonia asking him to come and help him. (Acts 16:9) Just as that dream prompted a change in his ministry journey, this dream changed mine.

I will share the dream in its entirety and then respond to various questions it raises. I have spent countless hours, months and years seeking biblical insight and historical perspective in order to even begin to write. The thoughts and insights presented have not been formed in haste. Rather, because of the seriousness of the dream, I brought the matter time and again before the Lord, and continue to feel the pressing weight of its importance, given where we are on God's timetable. I trust the Lord will give you wisdom and discernment to test the spirit with which this is written, and see whether these things are to be passed down to your children and grandchildren.

My earnest prayer is that He, in whose service I have desired to write *Letters To Aleeyah,* would graciously accept the humble service…to forgive what is mistaken and bless what is true.

THE DREAM: "Contract In Arial"
(August 16, 2009)

(As I wrote it in my journal after awaking.)
A black woman asked for my help in negotiating and writing up a contract spelling out the terms of an agreement regarding custody of her children.

She was very wealthy.

In the dream, I was trying to make sure everything was in the correct font…I was trying to find Arial, because for some reason that was what was needed. I had to fix the contract manually because some words kept ending up gobbledygook, so there were times where the work was very tedious, making sure each word was in the right font.

The woman and her children and I were watching this contract come together. With each word properly formatted, we could literally see an "army of warriors" being loaded into the document. However, if the font were other than Arial, enemy forces would load. Thus, one of the main themes of the dream was that **the contract had to be in Arial!**

End of dream.

Key Principles of Dream Interpretation To Consider

1. God loves to speak in pictures. (parables, symbols, types, shadows) This is an Eastern style of communication, meaning it is indirect, not the bullet point, "in your face" style that Westerners prefer. We want God to just tell it like it is, point blank…whereas He prefers to see how we respond to His message, the little bit that He initially gives. Will we ignore it? Or will we search the matter out? It is the latter that God desires. Proverbs 2:3-4 says, *"If you cry out for insight and raise your voice for understanding, if you seek it like silver and search for it as for hidden treasures; then you will understand the fear of the Lord and find the knowledge of God."* It honors Him when we follow Jesus' exhortation to *"take heed to what you hear."* (Mark 4:24)

2. Identify the main characters in the dream, especially the part you (The Dreamer) play, for a dream typically says something about your calling. In this dream, we have two women: a wealthy black woman with many children who is seeking help…and me. Thus, I have a choice as to how I will respond: 1) Ignore this woman's request and go on with my life; or 2) Press in and seek understanding in what she needs, and how I can help her.

3. Ask questions pertinent to the dream. For example: Why was she coming to me? Why was she a black woman and not another race? Is the answer significant? What problem is she having with custody of her children? Why does she think I can help her with that? What does Arial mean? Yes, it is a popular font, but what does that have to do with anything? Where was the focus of the dream? In other words, what specific action was being emphasized or "highlighted" by the Lord?

Those were the initial questions I had as I brought this dream before the Lord off and on over a period of many months as the dream dangled in my spirit. Because I believe the Lord desires to communicate to more of His children in dreams and visions, allow me to take you behind the curtain of unlocking the meaning of this dream. *[Note: The full interpretation did not come to light in ten minutes! In my experience, a "God dream" is typically one with many layers of meaning. They take time to get into your spirit.]*

Unlocking The Dream

Why was it a black woman asking for my help?

Ever since 1986 when I was inspired to write a black musical, I have suffered things a lot of black women experience: divorce, the struggle of being a single mom, racial discrimination, family turmoil, financial challenges, widowhood and growing up with little personal affirmation from my father. Additionally, over the years, I have observed that those who have resonated most with my work have been African-American women.

Just recently, I received the following response from a new reader. It touched me deeply. She wrote, *"Thank you for hearing my heart. I have read your monograph on the "Sexual Assault on the Church." I commented to a friend who heard you speak at a women's conference that your words seem to wrap around my heart and pull me higher. Your sensitivity to the experiences of African-Americans has a deeply healing and liberating effect. I have, over the last two years, fallen back into the struggle with purity as has every single one of my African-American sisters. We are desperate for our freedom and for those that follow. It feels like what you are saying is a unifying agent that pulls together the many words spoken over my life and helps to bring clarity to why I have had such struggles even though I have loved Jesus since I was six."*

I was deeply humbled by her letter. Suddenly the "black woman in the dream" came to life. She was real flesh and blood pouring out her heart. Like the woman in the dream – whom I named **Aleeyah** – she was pleading for her and her children's freedom. I am thankful that He is somehow using my writing to bring inner healing and freedom and pray this book meets with a similar response!

Why did this woman trust me to help her?

I dedicated my book, *The Levitical Calling*, to my sisters of color. You see, when I was so broken after losing almost everything in a business venture that collided with the events surrounding 9-11, God used many women of color in my life. They didn't know I was a composer, or a writer and producer involved in the entertainment industry. All they knew was that I was deeply wounded and needed to heal. I was utterly broken; and though I had walked faithfully with the Lord since 1969, I had no answers to why He had allowed this in my life. I was spiritually mute. Over the next several years, I witnessed firsthand the power behind the prayers of my sisters of color. Many came alongside and shouldered my burdens. They were warriors in the spirit praying for me to come back to life. I will be eternally grateful.

In 2005, the Lord showed me in a dream that He was bringing His children of color to their time of leadership. My role in that dream was simply to articulate (in words) what they "knew in their spirit – that this was their time! During a ministry trip to Kenya, I prophesied the dream's importance at a church where I was speaking. Though the people struggled with incredible poverty, the depth of their spiritual hunger moved me. With tears running down my face, I prophesied, *"This is your time in history. God is calling you to help lead us in this evil day. You have been through so much hardship ...and He is going to use it all to help us fight the spiritual battles that are ahead. You have learned how to dig in, how to war against the devil, and survive. White people don't know how to do this. Life has been too easy for us...we are wusses...we don't have the caliber of strength that you do to fight in the day that's coming. You must take your place of leadership. We need you!"*

After the service, the First Lady (niece to the former King of Uganda) came up and said, *"Did you see me crying when you were speaking?"*

I said, *"No, I didn't. Why were you crying?"*

She replied, *"The Lord showed me the very same thing two years ago, and now He brings a white woman all the way to Kenya to confirm it to me!"*

Wow...God is an awesome God!

In still another dream, I was walking down the street in front of a university campus. One student stood out – a young African-American woman – motioning for me to come inside. I reluctantly walked inside, thinking (in the dream), *"What am I doing here?*

They've already got teachers…there is no place for me here." As the woman took me through several classrooms, she pointed to the stairs and said, *"The personnel office is on the third floor."* (i.e., the third heaven)

I bring this up simply to illustrate that the Lord uses consistent and repetitive pictures (dreams, visions, a "knowing") to point the way to our calling. Dreams plant seeds of destiny into our spirit…and they bear fruit in their season. I was reminded yet again that He did have something for me to say to women of color, and He would call it forth in His time. Remember, when God was preparing Joseph for what He was to become, He gave him more than one dream saying the same thing. I'm not comparing myself to Joseph, mind you. I'm drawing your attention to a principle in dream interpretation. The Lord is <u>always</u> speaking to our spirits, and does so in many ways. It is up to us to "take heed to those messages." Think back to some of your dreams. Believe me, He has been showing you scenes consistent with your calling as well.

Lastly, the Lord has shown me over and over since 1986 the high calling of African-Americans. I believe He knew He could trust me to speak into Aleeyah's life.

Why was the woman wealthy? Is that a significant detail?
Absolutely, it is significant. It shows the black woman from God's perspective. He endowed her with great wealth, a strong anointing, and an awesome mandate to shepherd the next generation…but more than that. Not just any generation, but *this* generation…a generation that is very important to God. There are scriptures involving His children of color waiting to be fulfilled. He is taking them to a higher dimension that they ever thought possible. God wanted me to "see her through His eyes." In her own eyes, she may be struggling as a single mom with limited finances and getting nowhere in her own personal dreams…yet she was front and center in my dream…and in His heart. It was all about her. He heard her cries for her children. He knew their struggles to be free from bondage.

What does the Arial font have to do with it?
Unlocking that meaning was truly an a-ha moment for me. It is incredibly exciting to experience Holy Spirit at key moments of revelation. I devote an entire chapter to this question.

What is this custody agreement?
That took a long time for me to understand. I deal with this issue in more depth as well.

Why did I name the woman Aleeyah?
I wanted an African name, because that is the origin of the people of color...but one that is associated more with Ethiopia and Hebrew as opposed to a Muslim connotation. The name *Aleeyah* (as well as derivations such as *Aliyah, Lia, Leah*) is from the Amharic/Biblical Semitic language spoken in Ethiopia. I chose it because of a scripture yet to be fulfilled in Zephaniah 3:10,13 *"From beyond the rivers of Ethiopia my suppliants, the daughter of my dispersed ones, shall bring my offering. On that day you shall not be put to shame...for they shall pasture and lie down, and none shall make them afraid."* The name *Aliyah*, and its derivation *Lia*, mean "bringer of the gospel." In Hebrew, the word means "ascent" or "going up." When a Jew makes *aliyah*, he or she immigrates or returns to the land of Israel.

As we delve into the early history of our ancestors, hopefully this will all make beautiful sense. The Lord is calling us to oneness, and to cling to Him for the wonderful purpose He has for our lives.

What is the format of the book?
In the dream, the woman asks for my help regarding an important issue related to the freedom of future generations of her people. The very custody of her children is at stake. Her children need to know who their Father is and have a legal document to stand on that He will care for them.

Toward that end, my study centered on the early history of our spiritual ancestors. We all stemmed from Adam...then from Noah...and then spiritually from Abraham. But what really happened in all that? Why did some people groups seem to flourish, (like White people)...and the Jews and Blacks go from one hardship to another? Are the latter two connected in some way?

My historical quest involved not only the teachings of Scripture, but also several works of antiquity that were highly regarded by our spiritual forefathers. Primary among them:

- The <u>Ancient Book of Jasher</u>, which is referenced in Joshua 10:13; 2 Samuel 1:18; and 2 Timothy 3:8 as a revered historical record of God's people.

- The <u>Book of Enoch</u>, which details what happened when the Watchers (angels assigned to care for mankind) rebelled against the Most High God, left their watch and commingled their seed with earthly women, producing a hybrid race referred to as Nephilim in Genesis 6. This demonically-infused race peopled the known world prior to the Flood. Scripture tells us that when the Flood took place, only Noah and his family were untainted. Think about that: only eight people with untainted blood! The iniquity introduced by the Nephilim was so widespread and abhorrent to the Lord that He brought about the Flood to wash the earth clean of demonic filth. Thereby, humanity would begin anew, and these eight people would safeguard the purity of the blood-line from whose seed the Savior and Redeemer of the world would come.

- <u>The Antiquities of the Jews</u> by Flavius Josephus, a first century priest who later became the commander of Jewish forces in Galilee following the revolt against Rome. Most scholars agree that no source, other than the Bible itself, provides more relevant information on the history of the Jewish people and life during the first century.

There were many other books I consulted which are listed in the Bibliography. I do not claim to be a historian or a scholar. My primary objective was to help Aleeyah in her quest to construct the tightest custody agreement for her children, *"to give them a future and a hope."* (Jeremiah 29:11)

Examination of the Past

I went back to the beginning: How did the races begin? Why were Blacks and Jews so persecuted of all the people groups? Why have so many struggled during their lives? Did they share something in common? Are there historical reasons why many people of color have eluded true freedom? Are there open doors that the enemy has exploited to oppress them? If so, what are they…and how can these doors be closed?

I have done my best to dig through the biblical and historical evidence and present findings I hope will point to a gateway of freedom for a people whose time has come.

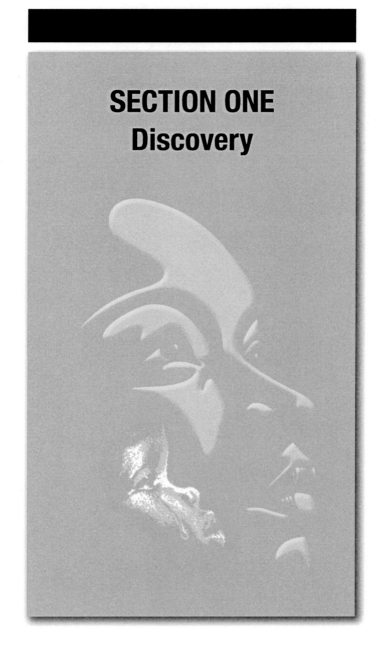

SECTION ONE
Discovery

LETTER 1
The Legal Process

Dear Aleeyah,

I am humbled that you appealed to me in a dream. I have seen your tears and listened to your heartache for your children. I have taken seriously your plea for my help, and have done the best I know how to make sense of why injustices continue to be perpetrated on so many of your children. Like you, I have been very perplexed…because the Lord showed me a long time ago that He is bringing people of color into critical leadership positions for the difficult days ahead.

Things I uncovered in my research have both startled and enlightened me. Some things have been deeply disturbing. I discovered layers of pain you have had to endure that frankly, I did not know existed. How much those hurts grieve the Father. Ultimately, however, the discovery journey has given me hope, because I see a bright light at the end of a long journey you and your children were asked to take.

In these letters, I will address the heart of your plea: namely, "writing up a contract spelling out the terms of an agreement regarding custody of your children."

What Is A Contract?

Since I saw the contract in the dream, I had to go to the Lord for clarification. Why was it a *contract*? First of all, a contract is a legal document that addresses all areas of the Law relative to a child custody issue, and is binding when executed properly. The Lord is not talking about "Law" as it relates to governmental laws. Rather, He is referring to the spiritual laws He put into place that govern His children and instruct us in His ways.

The 613 specific laws contained in the Old Testament were written for our instruction as well as our protection. Some of these laws affect only each individual and the time period in which he or she lives. In other instances, however, breaking a law by a person in one generation can affect multiple generations down the line, even if that person is unaware of what an ancestor might have done. For example, the fifth commandment *"Honor thy father and thy mother, so that you may live long in the land…,"* (Exodus 20:12) is a law with a built-in consequence and affects each one of us. If we dishonor or judge either mother or father in an area, we effectively sow a "bitter root judgment" into our spirit and the spiritual law of Sowing and Reaping goes into effect. We will reap that judgment at some point in the future.

You might ask, *"How do you know when a bitter root judgment has occurred?"*

You will learn to spot it in someone's life over time. It could be affecting you…or one of your children. A good rule of thumb is when you see the same bad thing cropping up: consistently losing jobs, multiple marriage breakups, unwanted pregnancies, etc. It is the *repetitive* pattern you are looking for. Let's say one of your children is always broke because every time he or she steps out into a new job or business venture, some crisis happens and everything falls apart. If this becomes a consistent pattern, it is a clear sign that a bitter root judgment may have been sown sometime in the past. This happens with everyone. Learning to spot these signs and break the cycle is a sign of spiritual maturity, when you can help another to search the matter out and bring all unknown or forgotten sins before the Lord through confession and repentance.

On the other hand, take the second commandment, *"You shall not make for yourself an image in the form of anything in heaven above or on the earth beneath…you shall not bow down to them or worship them; for I, the Lord your God, am a jealous God, punishing the children for the sin of the parents to the third and fourth generation of those who hate me, but showing love to a thousand generations of those who love me and keep my commandments."* (Exodus 20:4-6) [Emphasis mine]

When someone in one generation bows the knee to another god, it has devastating consequences to somebody three or more generations later. You say, *"That's unfair."* It may seem like that…but we must see that if it were no big deal, the Lord would not have it as one of the Ten Commandments. I personally have experienced reaping an ancestor's sinfulness…and have witnessed it in countless others. I will cover this in more detail in the chapter called *"The Need For Generational Cleansing."* It is that important. In fact, I believe this is one of the most important spiritual disciplines needed today, and one of the least understood.

In this book, we will examine "matters of the Law" that have the power to negatively impact our children's freedom. God's desire is to bless His children…always bless. But when there has been a deliberate or unknown disregard for His Laws somewhere in the generations, the consequences will be very evident. He wants us to learn how to spot the signs, help our children repent, and receive the forgiveness made available through our Lord's sacrifice.

In any legal matter, here are the parties and our respective roles:

DEFENDANT:	You
DEFENSE ATTORNEY:	Me
THE PROSECUTOR:	Satan
THE JUDGE:	The Lord Most High
THE LAWS:	The Old & New Testaments

Things To Remember

The Judge is Good, Faithful, Merciful, Righteous, Loving and Just. But, He honors His Word, which includes laws, ordinances, statutes, precepts and commandments revealed in the Old Testament, and everything His Son taught. Our arguments and appeals have to be based on His revealed Word, for He honors it when we seek to follow His ways. He is the Redeemer, and is glorified in every act of redemption. That's what we are asking Him for: your redemption and that of your children. Remember, He left the ninety-nine and went looking for the lost one. (Luke 15:1-6) That is His heart…and it's important that you know this going into His court. The Word says, *"The Lord executes righteousness and judgment for all that are oppressed."* (Psalms 103:6)

The Prosecutor knows when every Law has been compromised, and he is quick to accuse you and your children. He sees every mistake anyone has ever made. He has detailed records: times, dates, places, and millions of "witnesses" who think nothing of lying just to see your case fall apart. He will try to intimidate you. Do not be alarmed. That's who he is: a liar whose ultimate aim is to kill and destroy your children before they can be redeemed.

My goal is to provide you with ammunition for a proper Defense and work with you to word the custody agreement based on the Law. In order to do that, we first have to go through the Discovery process. We need to examine their "evidence." We will especially zero in on any possible old covenants or ancestral vows.

I believe you will find the Discovery fascinating. I uncovered a gold mine of revelation and promises hidden within the biblical and historical archives of our ancestors. Important keys to our defense lie there.

Our Secret Strategy

If the Prosecutor brings up evidence that hits home and you know in your heart that you or your children were guilty in that point of Law, you can address the court right then and there and admit guilt in that matter. Then you plead with the Judge for mercy on that point of Law, because of the price His Son paid for that sin.

That is my cue to make a Motion To Suppress that evidence…and once he agrees to Suppress That Evidence, your admission of guilt can no longer be read into the record… EVER!

LETTER 2
Remember The Final Scene

Dear Aleeyah,

Before exploring our ancestral history, I want you to consider where we are going in all this. I am a screenwriter…and one critical technique of the screenwriting craft is that the writer should always have the final scene emblazoned in her mind, and then write every scene and every character's dialogue in such a way as prepares the viewer to fully resonate with that scene. In fact, the final scene, if it's well written, is the *glory* of the film.

This is exactly what God does. He has written the entire redemption story… *"declaring the end from the beginning."* (Isaiah 46:10) He formed you and your people before the foundation of the world, for a noble purpose…for a gold chalice, not a crumpled tin cup in a homeless shelter.

Jesus endured the cross for the joy of the *glory* set before Him. (Hebrews 12:2) The Apostle Paul wrote while in prison before his death, *"I have fought the good fight, I have finished the race, I have kept the faith. Henceforth there is laid up for me the crown of righteousness, which the Lord, the righteous judge, will award to me on that Day."* (2 Timothy 4:7-8) Scripture teaches that there are hard times in life, many hardships and trials, but *"if we endure, we shall also reign with him."* (2 Timothy 2:12)

Suffering Is Part Of Our Calling

When the mother of John and James asked if her sons could sit on His right and left in the Kingdom, the Master answered, *"You do not know what you are asking. Are you able to drink the cup that I am to drink?"* (Matthew 20:22)

There was a cup given to the Messiah. It was part of His calling. The cup was filled with pain, grief, sorrow, betrayal, accusations, persecution, and finally death. He knew this going into His assignment…and He drank it willingly. If we walk with Him, and are called to serve Him, we must understand that suffering comes with the calling. It is the Messiah's life in us that is being attacked, not ours.

The Higher the Calling…the Greater the Suffering

In like manner, a cup of suffering was given you and your children. I have come to believe that because your people have such an important role to play in the Last Days, you were asked to endure greater hardship and trials than others. Paul said, *"For this cause I suffer these things."* (2 Timothy 1:12)

I have often pondered the mystery that of all people groups, the two that have suffered the most are Jews and Blacks. Later in the book, you will see how parallel their paths have been. My study has led me to conclude that each has such an important role to play in the redemptive plan of Almighty God in the Last Days that the demonic assault against them has been horrific.

I Was Shown Your Purpose In A Dream

It was August, 2004. I was still in my own wilderness period following 9-11. What follows is the dream itself, followed by notes from my journal as the Lord unlocked the meaning.

> ### THE DREAM: "Helping The Conductor"
> (August, 2004)
>
> A black man was practicing conducting *"The Lord's Prayer,"* and I was singing along so he would have a lyrical frame of reference as to where he was in the musical score.

That's it: two lines of description. And yet, two and a half pages of prophetic revelation poured forth from this dream. God used the dream to help me understand more fully my own calling…but most importantly for you, He showed me one of His intended purposes for His children of color.

Let's break out the dream together.

The Conductor:

In the "cast of characters," it was a black man conducting, not a white man, or a Jew, or any other race. Aleeyah, he represents a primary calling of your people in the Last Days. First of all, notice that he was the *conductor*. Not the tuba player, or the man who sweeps up after rehearsal. He was the <u>man</u>!...the head honcho given the awesome responsibility of bringing multitudes of instruments and voices into a unified living, breathing symphony of praise to the Lord.

In the dream, I noticed that he conducted the orchestra by "feel," not by sight. He was learning as he went. He was tentative in what he was doing. He probably never had formal conducting lessons...or much understanding of choral and orchestral scores. What he did know, however, with everything inside of him, was that he was supposed to pick up the baton and lead a group of musicians and a choir. That inner knowing burned inside of him...that same kind of "knowing" Moses had that he was to lead his people out of Egypt. Regardless whether the conductor was confident that he could do this, he poured his heart out doing it nonetheless...swinging that baton for all he was worth.

I observed no pride nor pomp in this man. He even allowed a white woman to sing along, so he would know where he was in the music. You see, chances are, the "experienced, trained conductors" had been removed from the church long before... having swelled up with pride and self-exaltation to such a degree the Almighty could no longer use them. So, what does the Lord do? He brings forth new leaders like this one, with no self-concept of grandeur. Rather, they tremble in the magnitude of the assignment because they are awed by the calling and the responsibility they sense, not only for their people...but most of all, to bring forth a praise befitting the Most High God. Humility and brokenness: the two qualifications necessary for a worship leader's resume in these Last Days.

My Role:

As an aside, Aleeyah, 80% of all dreams you have will be *intrinsic* in nature...meaning, they show you something about <u>your</u> calling. They are all about <u>you</u>. In like manner, this dream showed me something of mine. This dream, in fact, was used by God to help me understand my foreordained purpose. My role was not to lead. It was not to take over and show the conductor how it was done. Rather, my role was using words (i.e., lyrics) to help him keep his place. It didn't matter to him that I was white. He simply needed an understanding of what stirred in his heart. My gifting and calling are in the articulation of words that help bring awareness of destiny and purpose to His children of color. Most of my life since 1986 has been dedicated to that purpose.

Practicing:

The conductor was *practicing*. This wasn't the final performance. This was a time of practice, of memorizing the music, every nuance of the music, of learning how to direct an orchestra and choir (many different voices and instruments) for God's glory. I'm sure you see this…I see it too, how so many men and women of color are being raised up now in the pulpit, teaching God's Word and ministering through music. They are all over the Billboard charts in the Gospel Music industry. And yes, sadly, many are being lured away by the lusts of the flesh and the lure of fame. This is all part of the practice period…the purging away of those who no longer desire God's glory, but rather their own…ones who want to be served the offering plate more than offering themselves to serve others. But remember, we're still in the "practice time." God is still going to be God!

The Lord's Prayer:

This was the selection that he was asked to conduct. It is His prayer, and His desire, that a black man conduct it. Just ponder that for a moment: *"It is His prayer and desire that a black man conduct the final anthem!"* We'll see why in a moment.

It is also the Lord's prayer that a black man and a white woman work together, representative of true reconciliation and unity: in race, and in gender. Just as the Conductor has his call and his assignment, I have mine. We are to work together. In fact, I have observed that many white people often have words, but no heart. And black people often have heart, but no words. We need each other! The Conductor needed what I brought to the scene to fully function in his calling. And without his conducting leadership, my role would be totally unnecessary.

The Lyric:

There's one final detail the Lord provided: the specific lyric that I was singing in the dream, *"And lead us not into temptation, but deliver us from evil."* The way God speaks through pictures is incredible!

Why is this lyric so important? It tells us the time and season when this musical performance will be needed: the times we are entering now...the time Jesus spoke of in Luke 22:53b when He addressed Satan working through Judas. Jesus said, *"But this is your hour, and the power of darkness."*

Why The Black Church Has Been Targeted For Defilement

The one thing that will bring us safely through these dark days is the pure voice of praise and worship...multi-racial voices in harmony with one another. The devil cannot function in an atmosphere of true worship...but it must be pure. It must be undefiled. This is why there has been such a sexually defiling onslaught aimed strategically at the Black Church. The enemy knows his time is short. He also knows the Black Church is being raised up for this time...sounds of praise coming from the altars of Black Churches.

SUGGESTED PRAYER
"Holy Father, I thank You that You have a wonderful purpose for me and my children in these Last Days. I ask that You purge us of every defiling spirit that would keep us from our intended destiny. In Jesus' name, amen.

LETTER 3
The Contract In "Arial"

Dear Aleeyah,

This was such a critical part of the dream that I want to devote an entire section to it. Let me review it:

THE DREAM: "Contract In Arial"
(August 16, 2009)

(As I wrote it in my journal after awaking.)
A black woman asked for my help in negotiating and writing up a contract spelling out the terms of an agreement regarding custody of her children.

She was very wealthy.

In the dream, I was trying to make sure everything was in the correct font…I was trying to find Arial, because for some reason that was what was needed. I had to fix the contract manually because some words kept ending up gobbledygook, so there were times where the work was very tedious, making sure each word was in the right font.

The woman and her children and I were watching this contract come together. With each word properly formatted, we could literally see an "army of warriors" being loaded into the document. However, if the font were other than Arial, enemy forces would load. Thus, one of the main themes of the dream was that **the contract had to be in Arial!**

End of dream.

Interpretive Principle: God Uses Vocabulary Familiar To The Dreamer

A dream or vision is filled with metaphorical or pictorial language: words that convey layers of meaning. Because Holy Spirit is speaking, and because His desire is to communicate very personally with the dreamer, He will use words, phrases and concepts the dreamer understands.

In this section of the dream, He used three concepts I (as the Dreamer) understand:

Concept #1: He told this story using a writer's terminology in terms of context, layout, fonts and graphic design. I founded my ad agency in 1983. For years, my work has involved designing, editing and manually manipulating individual words, making sure the fonts are consistent and the document is laid out accurately according to the rules of the particular document in question. My profession as a writer demands that when I am writing or editing something, I have to zoom in to each word and examine it both contextually (*Does it make sense?*) and aesthetically (*Does it look right?*). It is not uncommon for me to re-read a sentence ten or twenty times, examining each word. Thus, this dream spoke my language.

Concept #2: As an professional wordsmith, I look at what the Speaker (in this case, Holy Spirit) is trying to say. How does He use pictures or words to emphasize a point? For example, there is a Hebraic principle where repeating a word or the use of another word that means the same thing brings emphasis. When Jesus says, *"Truly, Truly,"* this is a verbal cue for the listener to pay attention to what comes next, because to God, that next thing is very important! In like manner, with this dream, the word *Arial* kept coming up. I immediately saw it as a point of emphasis God was bringing to my attention. Therefore, I became even more intent to discover what He meant by the word.

Concept #3: God often uses what's called a "play-on-words," where a word or phrase says one thing, but means another. For example, when Jesus said, *"Unless you eat the flesh of the Son of man and drink his blood, you have no life in you..."* (John 6:53), Jesus was not promoting cannibalism and vampires. He was speaking metaphorically, in words that mean one thing literally, but a whole different meaning contextually. In like manner, Holy Spirit wasn't really talking about the importance of Arial as a typeface...as if this contract would be null and void if it were in Times New Roman. No. He was using a common "play-on-words" or "sound-a-like" to uncover His meaning. As I looked at the dream and re-read it over and over, He drew my attention to a word that "sounded like" Arial, but had a whole *other* meaning…<u>Ariel</u>. This is where the Holy Spirit downloaded the "a-ha" moment. When I wrote down the word *Ariel*, suddenly God's revelation flooded my spirit. I <u>knew</u> what He was saying!

Interpretation Notes

I looked up *Ariel* in both <u>Strong's Concordance</u> and Merrill F. Unger's <u>Bible Dictionary</u>. Here's what I found: *Ariel* has two distinct meanings:

> <u>**#1**</u> The word *Ariel* is the symbolic name for Jerusalem. You'll find it in Isaiah 29:1. *"Woe to Ariel, the city where David dwelt!"* The Hebrew word is composed of two parts: *'ariy*, which means "lion of God, heroic, lion-like men" and *'el*, which is a shortened form of *'ayil*, which means anything strong, specifically a political chief or a mighty man.

> A font is the appearance of the wording in such a way that gives it declarative power. Arial was what was called for in this contract, for *Ariel* is the "lion of God," an army of warriors that will come to your defense. The Lord was pointing out the secret weapon that is available to you and your descendants if we write your custody agreement contract "in the spirit of Ariel," aligned with the Laws that the Most High gave His people, the Jews.

> Look again at what the dream communicated: *"With each word properly programmed in Arial, we could see an 'army of warriors' being loaded."*

> This nightly revelation was a "word of wisdom" dream in which the Lord instructed me how to word this contract, and where the strength and authority of it would be found. What He is saying, Aleeyah, is that <u>if</u> this contract aligns with what God has revealed in His Word, and addresses every point of the Law that affects the custody of your children, you and I will witness an unseen force of warriors – the likes of which we have never seen – fighting on your and their behalf!

What a powerful truth…and promise from the throne room!

#2 The second use of the word *Ariel* is found in Ezra 8:16. Ariel was one of the leaders of Jews in captivity in Persia that was sent by Ezra to call forth the Levites to enlist them for service in rebuilding the Temple, the place God chose to dwell in the earth.

When Ezra was given permission and monetary aid from King Cyrus of Persia to return to Jerusalem and rebuild the ruined Temple, this band of some 1,514 Jews that volunteered to go stopped midway to take stock of itself. Ezra records his shocking discovery: *"I gathered them to the river that runs to Ahava, and there we encamped three days. As I reviewed the people and the priests, I found there none of the sons of Levi."* (Ezra 8:15) [Emphasis mine]

No Levites?! They could not rebuild Temple without the Levites! Where were they?

Ezra continues, *"Then I sent for Eliezer, Ariel, Shemaiah, Elnathan...leading men, and for Joiarib and Elnathan, who were men of insight, and sent them to Iddo, the leading man at the place Casiphia, telling them what to say to Iddo and his brethren the temple servants at the place Casiphia, namely, to send us ministers for the house of our God. And by the good hand of our God upon us, they brought us a man of discretion, of the sons of Mahli the son of Levi, son of Israel..."* (Ezra 8:16-18) [Emphasis mine]

I almost fell off the couch when I read this account. It spoke volumes to me. If you have read **The Levitical Calling,** you might see what excited me so. One of the "a-ha" moments of inspiration when writing that book came when I examined in detail the three families of the Levites: the Kohathites (sons of Kohath), Gershonites (sons of Gershon), and Merarites (sons of Merari).

In the diagram on the opposite page, you find the patriarch Levi, one of the twelve sons of Jacob. Levi had three sons, who comprised the three levitical families that guarded the Tabernacle as the Israelites made their way from Egypt to the Promised Land.

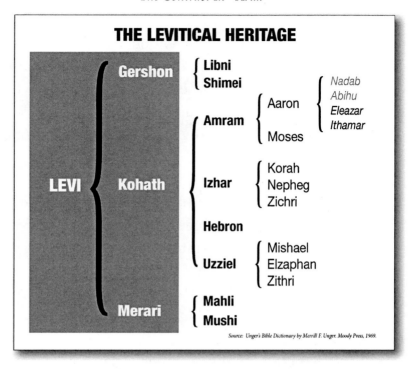

THE LEVITICAL HERITAGE

Source: *Unger's Bible Dictionary by Merrill F. Unger. Moody Press, 1969.*

As you see here, Merari had two sons...one of whom was Mahli, whose very descendant responded to Ezra's call for help in rebuilding the Temple! Aleeyah, I believe this is significant in bringing understanding concerning the destiny of your children in these Last Days.

As explained in more depth in *The Levitical Calling*, Merarites are Levites entrusted to build the proper foundation for a place where God desires to dwell. In Ezra's case, it was the Temple. Merarites are foundation experts...and in today's application of this new breed of Levites, Merarites are those Levites uniquely called to the Marketplace. We typically do not fit in with other Levites, because we have this unique "internal beacon" when God is expanding His tent "way over there!"

For example, while the Kohathites are deep in intercession and worship...while the Gershonites are maintaining order and being proper gatekeepers for where God is currently dwelling...the Merarites usually get the first inkling that God is about to pull up stakes and move someplace new!

This is what is happening now: God is calling the Church out of the pews and into the world, to become His Light there. In other words... He's calling Merarites!!! In this dream, that means He's calling many of your children to their Marketplace assignments!

Another thing I'd like to bring to your attention, Aleeyah, is that Ezra described someone from Mahli's clan as being gifted with the spirit of understanding. Mahli could <u>see</u> what God was doing in the earth at this key juncture in history. God was calling Mahli's family of Levites to rebuild, from the ruins, the foundations of where He desires His presence to dwell. Your children have a key place in God's heart for doing the same thing now, at this time in history!

Let me give you something to ponder: In the dream, the "Black Woman" (you) is crying out for the release of her children, to break the bondage they are in. This release can only be found in the power of verbal declaration that aligns with the people of Ariel… Jerusalem…the lion of God!

The timing for this release is NOW…which I believe relates to the call of Merarites among your children to take their places building a foundation of praise within their Marketplace assignment so that the Lord can dwell among His people and expand His Kingdom tent. Your function as a levitical people is a Merarite one….it is foundational to what is coming and what God is building in the earth!

Prophetically…Just as the command of God spoken through Moses released angelic power to affect the release of God's children from a captive land, so the prophetic release of the "spirit of Ariel" will go forth from you, Aleeyah, to effect freedom for this generation of people of color, who are called to help set up the tents of praise in the earth prior to the Lord's return.

The important takeaway from this dream is this: **the secret of strength lies in your spiritual alignment with our Jewish forefathers.** For Hebraic emphasis, let me say it another way: **The secret to your children's freedom lies in the *"Tent of Shem."***

SUGGESTED PRAYER
"Lord, I ask You to light the candle of understanding in my heart and give me the ability to discern Your truth regarding the things that are being disclosed in this book, especially regarding how to align with the Jewish people. In Jesus' name, amen."

LETTER 4
Uncovering Our Godly Ancestral Roots

Dear Aleeyah,

Following God's judgment in Genesis 3, the descendants of Adam and Eve went in two different directions:

1. Descendants of Seth who chose to follow the Lord and walk in His ways.
2. Those who harbored iniquity and followed Cain in rebellion against the Lord.

Your ancestors and mine chose to follow the Lord.

God's Message In The Names

As you see in the diagram on the next page, the godly line (from which Messiah would come) spanned over 1600 years before the Flood. The meaning of our forefathers' names reveals an incredible message, foretelling that One would come to redeem us from our fallen nature:

"It is appointed for mortal man to experience sorrow. But the Blessed God came down teaching us that His death shall bring the despairing comfort."

What an awesome God we serve!

The Patriarchal Mandate

There were hundreds of other children born to these patriarchs, most of whom lived over 900 years …and yet God singled out these ten and entrusted them with a Patriarchal Mandate: *Guard the purity of your seed, love the Lord your God with all your heart, seek to follow His ways, and pass that down to the next generation.* The very salvation and redemption of the entire world was at stake.

Timeline of the Patriarchs

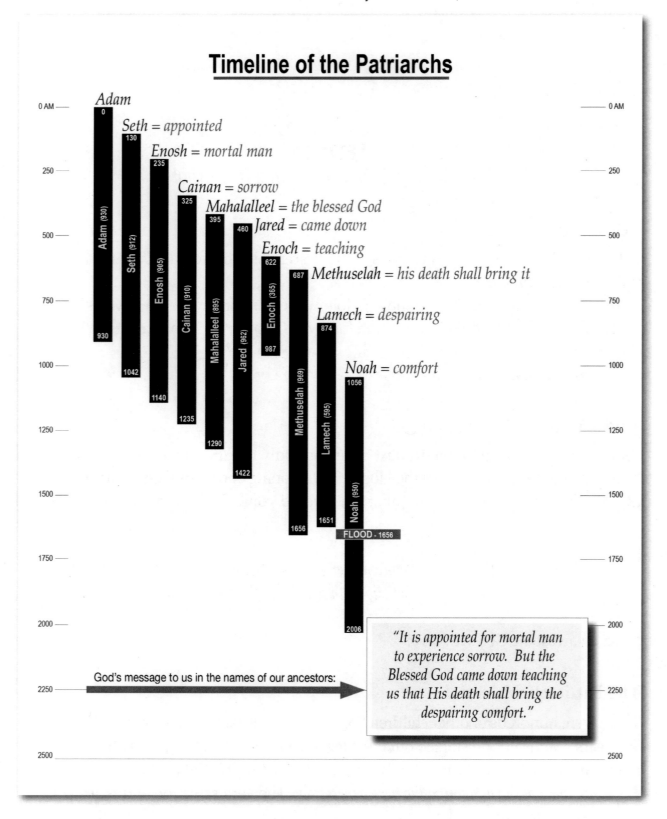

Adam

Seth = appointed

Enosh = mortal man

Cainan = sorrow

Mahalalleel = the blessed God

Jared = came down

Enoch = teaching

Methuselah = his death shall bring it

Lamech = despairing

Noah = comfort

God's message to us in the names of our ancestors:

"It is appointed for mortal man to experience sorrow. But the Blessed God came down teaching us that His death shall bring the despairing comfort."

Who Were The Patriarchs?

We learn very little about these men from Genesis 5...merely their names, their fathers, their sons, and how long each lived. I began looking for their "backstory" in the early works of antiquity to expand my own understanding...but also to find clues for your quest. Among the books that were highly regarded by our Jewish fathers: <u>The Ancient Book of Jasher</u>, <u>The Lost Book of Enoch</u>, the <u>Antiquities of the Jews</u> by Flavius Josephus, *The Secrets of Enoch* and *The First and Second Books of Adam and Eve* which are sections in <u>The Lost Books of Eden</u>.

Allow me to share selected passages with you. What follows actually represents months of pouring through these books. My prayer is that these patriarchs will come alive for you, as they did for me. Moreover, I hope you will see the incredible sacrifice each one made in order to honor, preserve and pass on the ways of the Most High God.

Seth:

When Adam and Eve were cast out of the Garden of Eden, early records show that they made their home near Eden in a cave, which became known as the Cave of Treasures. There they raised their children, and Adam spent his days praying and ministering before God, teaching His ways to His children.

When Adam died at 930 years of age, his body *"was wrapped and embalmed with sweet spices from sacred trees and laid on the eastern side of the inside of the Cave, the side of the incense, and placed in front of him a lampstand that kept burning."*[1]

All of his children wept over Adam and made offerings to God for one hundred and forty days. *"The Word of God came to Seth, the eldest among them, saying unto him, 'O Seth...As I was with thy father, so also shall I be with thee, until the fulfillment of the promise I made him – thy father saying, I will send My Word and save thee and thy seed.' But as to thy father Adam, keep thou the commandment he gave thee; and <u>sever thy seed from that of Cain thy brother.</u>'"*[2] [Emphasis mine]

Cain and his seed dwelt in the valley below the "mountain of God" where the Cave of Treasures was, and Seth became head of what was described as the most happy and just tribe of people who ever lived.

About Seth was written,

"Seth the elder, tall and good, with a fine soul, and of a strong mind, stood at the head of his people; and tended them in innocence, penitence, and meekness, and did not allow one of them to go down to Cain's children. But because of their own purity, they were named 'Children of God,' and they were with God, instead of the hosts of angels who fell; for they continued in praises to God, and in singing psalms unto Him, in the Cave of Treasures…they did not like earthly work, but gave themselves to heavenly things; for they had no other thought than praises, doxologies, and psalms unto God. Therefore did they at all times hear the voices of angels, praising and glorifying God…they sowed not, neither did they reap; they wrought no food for the body, not even wheat; but only offerings. They ate of the fruit and of trees well flavoured that grew on the mountain where they dwelt…Seth often fasted every forty days, as did also his eldest children…they were happy, innocent, without sudden fear, there was no jealousy, no evil action, no hatred among them. There was no animal passion; from no mouth among them went forth either foul words or curse…they constrained their children and their women every day in the cave to fast and pray, and to worship the most High God."[3]

As Seth aged and he was near unto death, he gathered his children and grandchildren around him and prayed over them and blessed them, *"and adjured them by the blood of Abel the just, saying, 'I beg of you, my children, not to let one of you go down from this Holy and pure Mountain.'"*[4]

Enosh:

Seth's eldest son took his father's place as spiritual head of the family of the Children of God. Enoch was twenty years old at the time. The plot thickens in the explosion of evil on the earth. *"By the time Enosh was eight hundred and twenty, Cain had a large progeny; for they married frequently, being given to animal lusts; until the land below the mountain was filled with them."*[5]

The <u>Ancient Book of Jasher</u> records that it was during Enosh's days that the *"sons of men began to multiply, and to afflict their souls and hearts by transgressing and rebelling against God…they served other gods…and made images of brass and iron, wood and stone, and they bowed down and served them."*[6]

Cainan:

As each Patriarch died, they were likewise embalmed and entombed in the family shrine. Thus, his successor would minister before the Lord on behalf of the Children of God before the presence of his ancestors.

> Jasher records that,
> *"Cainan was a very wise man and had understanding in all wisdom, and with his wisdom he ruled over spirits and demons. And Cainan knew by his wisdom that God would destroy the sons of men for having sinned upon earth, and that the Lord would in the latter days bring upon them the waters of the flood. In those days Cainan wrote upon tablets of stone, what was to take place in time to come, and he put them in his treasures."*[7]

Mahalalleel:

During his leadership, the sons of men became ever more corrupt. As he neared his death, he prophesied to his son, Jared,

> *"Hereafter there shall come a great destruction upon this earth on account of them [children of Cain]; God will be angry with the world and will destroy them with waters. But I also know that thy children will not hearken to thee, and that they will go down from this mountain and hold intercourse with the children of Cain, and that they shall perish with them. O my son! Teach them, and watch over them, that no guilt attach to thee on their account…fulfil thy ministry before them, until thou enterest into rest thyself."*[8]

Jared:

True to his father's prophetic word, most of Jared's children forsook the mountain and joined the sons of Cain in the valley. It was during his generation, in fact, that the Watchers (angels who were given the assignment by God to watch over the sons of men) left their heavenly estate and commingled their seed [i.e., had sex] with the daughters of men.

Many demonic manifestations took place during Jared's watch: apparitions, deception, and seduction. It was written, *"As Jared was standing like a lion before the bodies of his fathers, praying and warning his people, Satan envied him, and wrought a beautiful apparition, because Jared would not let his children do aught without his counsel."*[9]

In other words, Jared started out strong, but was unfamiliar with demonic seduction of this magnitude. In fact, at one point, he was seduced to such an extent that he ventured forth into the valley of Cain under the lie that the apparitions had been sent by Jared's forefathers.

When Jared saw the behavior of the children of Cain,
"His very soul wrenched itself from them; neither would he taste of their food or of their drink…he wept, and then spread his hands and prayed with a fervent heart, and with much weeping, and entreated God to deliver him from their hands. No sooner did Jared begin to pray than the elder [Satan] fled with his companions; for they could not abide in a place of prayer…He wept and prayed, 'Send Thy angel to draw me out of the midst of them; for I have not myself power to escape from among them.'"[10]

In His mercy, God sent His angel to lead Jared back up the mountain, but when he returned to the Cave, he found the bodies of his ancestors thrown about and the lamp put out. Jared was heartbroken that he had failed in his guardianship of the Children of God.

Although the Lord forgave Jared and he was able to rekindle the lamp that shed light on the body of Adam, his children and grandchildren nonetheless began to go down from the holy mountain to mix with the children of Cain. Jared pleaded with tears and told them what would happen if they did,

"O my innocent and holy children, know that when <u>once you go down from this holy mountain, God will not allow you to return again to it</u>…the moment you leave it, you will be reft of life and of mercy; and you shall no longer be called 'children of God,' but 'children of the devil.' But they would not hearken to his words…When they looked at the daughters of Cain, at their beautiful figures, and at their hands and feet dyed with colour and tattooed in ornaments on their faces, the fire of sin was kindled in them…Satan also made the sons of Seth appear of the fairest in the eyes of the daughters of Cain, so that the daughters of Cain lusted after the sons of Seth like ravenous beasts…but after they had thus fallen into this defilement, they returned by the way they had come, and tried to ascend the Holy Mountain. But they could not, because the stones of that mountain were of fire flashing before them."[11]

Jared died in sorrow, but before he died, he called his son Enoch, grandson Methuselah and his son, Lamech, and great-great grandson Noah to his bedside and foretold of the days to come.

> *"Oh my sons, God will take you to a strange land, and ye never shall again return to behold with your eyes this garden and this holy mountain. Therefore, set your hearts on your own selves, and keep the commandment of God which is with you... unto him of you who shall be left shall the Word of God come and when he goes out of this land he shall take with him the body of our father Adam, and shall lay it in the middle of the earth, the place in which salvation shall be wrought.* <u>*Then Noah said unto him, 'Who is he of us that shall be left?' And Jared answered, 'Thou art he... and thy son Shem, who shall come out of thy loins, he it is who shall lay the body of our father Adam in the middle of the earth*</u>*...Then Jared turned to his son Enoch and said, "Thou, my son, abide in this cave, and minister diligently all the days of thy life; and feed thy people in righteousness and innocence...As Jared died, tears streamed down his face by reason of his great sorrow, for the children of Seth, who had fallen in his days."*[12] [Emphasis mine]

Personal Interjection

I want to pause a moment to reflect on the lives of our ancestors. I was deeply moved by their dedication to their parental responsibility to pray and intercede before God, amidst the growing evil that seduced their children and grandchildren. We battle not flesh and blood!

Aleeyah, I want to bring a matter to your attention that has burdened me greatly, for I see an important parallel to what we are experiencing now, with our generation. If any one thing has been a throughline of my life over the last twenty years, it has been the levitical compulsion to prepare others for the Kingdom of God.

I have spent many years pouring over books and scriptures relative to where we are in these Last Days. In *The Levitical Calling*, I brought forth the view embraced by our Jewish forefathers, and depicted the 7-Day Plan of God using the graph on the next page.

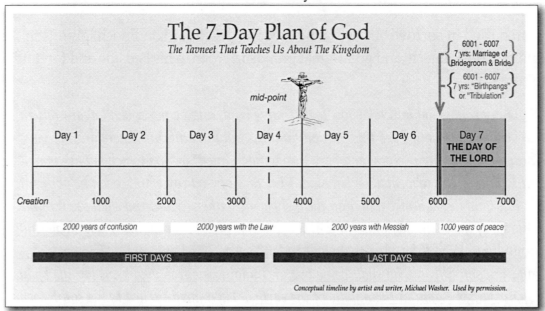

The 7th day is the day that is all Sabbath, the millennial rule of Messiah. As you can tell, we are fast approaching this Day! We are presently in Day 6, since 2012, at this writing, is the Hebrew year 5773 from Creation. What I see prophetically is that these 7 time periods parallel the 7 generations from Adam, as shown in the diagram below.

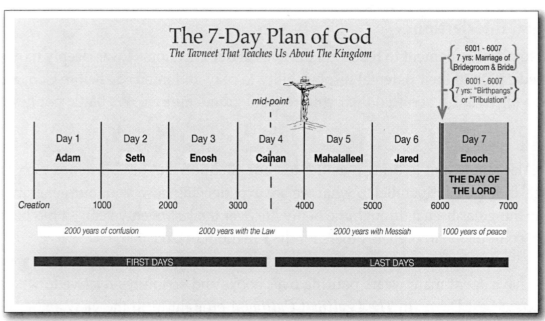

If I am correct, then we are in the generation of Jared, because he was the 6th patriarch from Adam. As you recall, it was during Jared's time that evil permeated the earth and the majority of the children of God left the holy mountain and joined the children of Cain in their wickedness.

What happens, though, in Day 7? The Bride of Christ goes "up" for 7 years during the Tribulation, and then we all come down to rule with Him for the remainder of the 1000-year Millenium.

What happened to Enoch, the 7th generation from Adam? He "went <u>up</u>!" The Lord uses the most brilliantly creative ways to give us "Pictures" – or in the Hebrew, the word is *tavniot* – to communicate what He is doing. He always prepares us for what is to come, when our spiritual eyes come into clearer focus.

As I was reflecting on what happened to the sons of men during Jared's leadership, it bore startling resemblance to our own time. We need to re-visit the days of Jared and hear again the warnings he gave to his generation, and what happened to them. I believe this is the warning we are to give our children, Aleeyah: *"If you go down the mountain, there is no escape…you will not be able to return."*

I have seen in dreams what Jared experienced, which I will share in full in a later chapter. In this dream, God clearly showed me that there is soon coming a time – if we're not already here – where the spirit of delusion will be so strong that the doors to the Church will be locked. Those inside, who have fallen to deception and defiling spirits, will not be able to escape. That was the admonition Jared gave his descendents: I liken the time of Jared as *"The Great Falling Away."* These are serious times we are living in.

Interestingly, the two patriarchs written about more than the rest were Jared and Enoch. I find this significant, given our unique time in history.

Enoch:

Enoch was sixty-five when he had Methuselah. Jasher records that,

> *"The soul of Enoch was wrapped up in the instruction of the Lord, in knowledge and in understanding; and he wisely retired from the sons of men and secreted himself from them for many days…the spirit of God was upon Enoch, and he taught all his men the wisdom of God and his ways, and the sons of men served the Lord all the days of Enoch and they came to hear his wisdom…they also required him to reign over them, to which he consented. Peace was on the earth throughout his life."*[13]

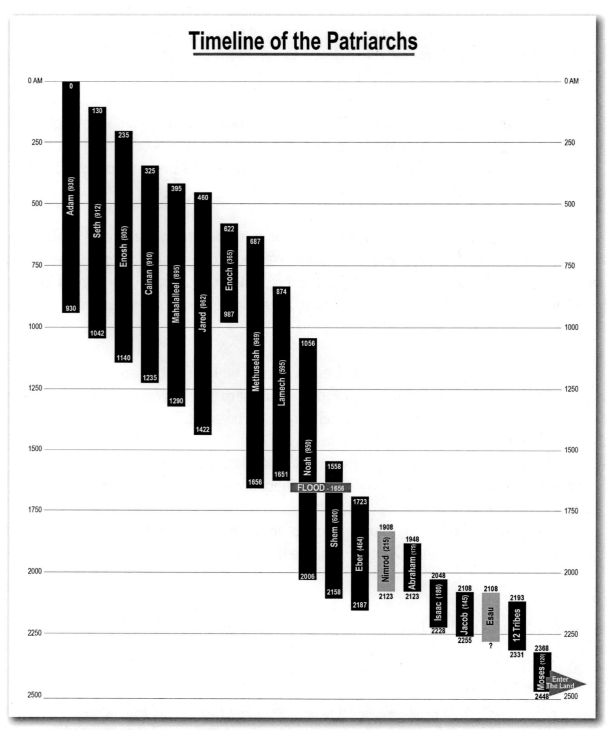

Timeline of the Patriarchs

We tend to look at these patriarchs in a linear way, one at a time. The reality is that because they lived so long, their lives overlapped. For instance, by the time Adam died, Enoch had been ruling for two hundred and forty-three years! They knew each other well. In fact, Enoch was spiritually mentored by Adam.

After Adam's death, Jasher writes that,

"Enoch resolved to separate himself from the sons of men and to secret himself as at first in order to serve the Lord...he kept away from the sons of men three days and then went to them for one day...and he did in this manner for many years, and afterward appeared to his people one day in seven; and after that once in a month, and then once in a year, until all the kings, princes and sons of men sought for him, and desired again to see the face of Enoch, and to hear his word; but they could not, as all the sons of men were greatly afraid of Enoch, and they feared to approach him on account of the Godlike awe that was seated upon his countenance."[14]

Time passed and:

"Enoch was teaching them the ways of God. Behold an angel of the Lord then called unto Enoch from heaven, and wished to bring him up to heaven to make him reign there over the sons of God, as he had reigned over the sons of men upon earth." Enoch then gathered his people and *"gave them divine instructions, and said, 'I have been required to ascend into heaven...and as he taught them, they lifted up their eyes and the likeness of a great horse descended from heaven, and the horse paced in the air...and stood before Enoch. He proclaimed, 'Where is the man who delighteth to know the ways of the Lord his God, let him come this day to Enoch before he is taken from us.' Eight hundred thousand men came to him."*[15]
[Emphasis mine]

Jasher records that when Enoch ascended into heaven, at age three hundred and sixty-five years, the people anointed his son Methuselah to reign over them. Methuselah, you may recall, lived longer than any other patriarch...969 years!

Enoch Was Referred To As God's Scribe

Enoch's writings were highly regarded by our Jewish forefathers. They were passed down the entire patriarchal line, and were found in the caves of Qumran. The Book of Enoch greatly influenced all of the writers of the New Testament.

Allow me to sum up a few things about this remarkable patriarch. Enoch was given a view of paradise, the many levels of heaven, and was shown the magnificent ways of God over a period of sixty days.

"The Lord summoned one of his archangels by name Pravuil, whose knowledge was quicker in wisdom than the other archangels, who wrote all the deeds of the Lord; and the Lord said to Pravuil: 'Bring out the books from my storehouses, and a reed of quick-writing, and give it to Enoch, and deliver to him the choice and comforting books out of thy hand. He told all the works of heaven, earth and sea, and all the elements, their passages and goings, and thunderings of the thunders, the sun and moon, the goings and changes of the stars, the seasons, years, days, and hours, the risings of the wind, the numbers of the angels, and the formation of their songs, and all human things, the tongue of every human song and life, the commandments, instructions, and sweet-voiced singings, and all things that it is fitting to learn. And Pravuil told me: 'All the things that I have told thee, we have written. Sit and write all the souls of mankind, however many of them are born, and the places prepared for them to eternity; for all souls are prepared to eternity, before the formation of the world.' And all double thirty days and thirty nights, and I wrote out all things exactly, and wrote three hundred and sixty-six books."[16]

Enoch's calling was like none other. He was chosen from all other men and designated as God's writer (or scribe) of all His creation.[17] After writing the 366 books, Enoch was sent back to his people to give them the books and instruct them in God's ways. He remained on earth thirty days and was again taken up to heaven where he will remain until the final period of the tribulation.[18]

Methuselah, Lamech & Noah:

You see from the Patriarchal Timeline that the last three generations prior to the Flood all lived during basically the same period. Everything Enoch learned from his heavenly visitation, he passed down to the three remaining righteous leaders on the earth.

During this same time, some 1300 – 1400 years after the Creation, the sons of men increased in evil upon the earth.

"Every man made unto himself a god, and they robbed and plundered every man his neighbor as well as his relative, and they corrupted the earth, and the earth was filled with violence…they took from the cattle of the earth, the beasts of the field and the fowls of the air, and taught the mixture of animals of one species with the other, in order to provoke the Lord…all flesh had corrupted its ways upon earth."[19]

We learn from Enoch that wickedness increased even more when the Watchers began to lust after the daughters of men. Two hundred of them *"descended in the days of Jared in the summit of Mount Hermon...they had sworn and bound themselves by mutual curses to carry out this plan and do this thing."*[20]

They left their angelic estate, married the women and produced a hybrid race referred to in Genesis 6 as Nephilim. These "giants, or mighty men of renown" brought such degradation and iniquity upon the earth that the Lord occasioned the Flood to destroy every living thing that was not on the ark with Noah.

SUGGESTED PRAYER
"Dear Lord, You are so holy and good to have infused our patriarchs with such devotion to You. I long for that level of closeness with You. Help me to be diligent to follow Your ways and pass them on to my children and grandchildren. Father, we live in such an evil day. Help me discern every spirit of defilement that would dare raise up against the knowledge of God and try to pervert the purity of my worship. In Jesus' name, amen.

LETTER 5
God Makes His Ways Known

Dear Aleeyah,

In studying our patriarchal ancestors, I came away with a much greater understanding of the sacrifices they made so that we could know the Lord.

Before the Scriptures were written down by Moses, the scribes and prophets, and then lived out by our Lord and His words written down by the apostles and passed down through the ages, "God's ways" were not available for everyone. I cannot imagine the sense of responsibility our forefathers felt, knowing the salvation of the world depended upon their faithfulness to pass down God's ways. Yet, isn't that what we should all feel – a burden to raise righteous children and grandchildren to pass on this great heritage of faith?

The Patriarchs After The Flood

We take for granted the knowledge of God and His ways, but in earlier times, our forefathers risked their lives for this knowledge.

Look at the following graph that depicts our ancestors following the Flood. Throughout the Bible, God refers to Himself as the God of Abraham, Isaac and Jacob... so these are the ones I want to especially highlight for you. This was the critical time, from God's perspective, of teaching His ways following the destruction of all flesh in the Flood.

Noah's Sons

Following the Flood, Noah's three sons peopled the entire known world: **Shem** (father of the Shemitic, or "Semitic" people), **Japheth** (father of the Caucasian, European and Asian nations) and **Ham** (father of people of color). You might be interested to learn that the Hebrew word *shem* means "name." God is often referred to by the Jews as *HaShem*, "The Name." Their entire identity as the "people of the Name" is to guard, revere and instruct the world in who He is.

If you look at the Patriarchal timeline after the Flood, you will see that Shem was the one commissioned to teach the world the ways of the Lord. Not Ham...nor Japheth. It was

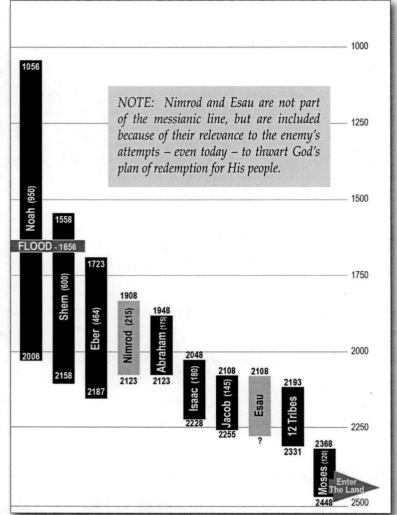

NOTE: *Nimrod and Esau are not part of the messianic line, but are included because of their relevance to the enemy's attempts — even today — to thwart God's plan of redemption for His people.*

not that God loved Shem more than your forefather or mine. It was Shem's calling. The Most High promised that His seed of righteousness would pass through the lineage of Shem, from whom Messiah would come. Shem's mandate, therefore, was to guard the purity of the Semitic bloodline. Having lived through the Flood and seen how God destroyed those whose blood was tainted by demonic seed, Shem undoubtedly felt the awesome responsibility to keep his bloodline pure. If it were tainted, Messiah could not come...and if that happened, mankind could not be redeemed.

As you read the historical accounts of God's people, you see the Father's constant admonition to wipe out the ungodly nations, and warn against intermarrying with tribes who did not know the Lord. The enemy was constantly at work to lure the Jews into false unions with godless neighbors whose blood was tainted.

The Origin of Black Jews

The late 20th century Emperor, Haile Selassie of Ethiopia was a man of color, and a descendent of Shem. In other words, he was a Black Jew.

The Semitic people [the Messianic line] includes Jews, Arabs, and the Amharic peoples who inhabited Ethiopia. You may recall that Solomon married the Queen of Sheba. Their child, Menelik I, [the first Jewish emperor of Ethiopia and ancestor of Emperor Selassie] often traveled to Jerusalem to visit his father, King Solomon.

For centuries the world's Jewish community was not even aware of these Ethiopian Jews who settled in the northern province of Gondar.

> *"Once they were kings. A half million strong, they matched their faith with fervor and out-matched the Moslem and Christian tribesmen around them to rule the mountain highlands around Lake Tana. They called themselves Beta Israel – the house of Israel – and used the Torah to guide their prayers and memories of the heights of Jerusalem as they lived in their thatched huts in Ethiopia. But their neighbors called them Falashas – 'the alien ones, the invaders.' And even three hundred years of rule, even the black features that matched those of all the people around them did not make the Jews of Ethiopia secure governors of their destiny in Africa."*[21]

If you go to Israel today, you will see many Black Jews. Over 8,000 Beta Israel (Falasha Jews) came to Israel between 1977 and 1984, but according to my sources, these efforts were nothing compared to the modern exodus that took place during 1984's *Operation Moses*, when wars and famines threatened Ethiopia. *"The miracle of Operation Solomon is only now being fully understood; an ancient Jewish community has been brought back from the edge of government-imposed exile and starvation. But once they were kings..."*[22]

The Mystery of the Ark of the Covenant

One theory holds that because Solomon feared for the safekeeping of the Ark of the Covenant, his son Menelik was given the real Ark to safeguard in Ethiopia while a copy remained in Jerusalem. Proponents of this theory, along with many devout Jews, believe that in the last days, before Messiah's return, the Ark will be uncovered by God from its centuries-old hiding place and restored to the Third Temple.

A story posted on June 25, 2009 in *WeeklyWorldNews.com* reported, *"Today, the Ethiopian Orthodox Church boasts that it [the Ark of the Covenant] sits under lock and key in the Chapel of the Tablet, near the Church of Our Lady Mary of Zion. It is only used occasionally in ritual processions, but almost no one has seen it, let alone gotten photographic evidence."* The report quoted the head of the Orthodox Church of Ethiopia as stating that the Ark of the Covenant will be revealed to the public.[23]

Some believe Zephaniah 3:10 references Ethiopian believers restoring the Ark to its intended home in Jerusalem, a true offering of praise, *"From beyond the rivers of Ethiopia my worshippers, my scattered people, will bring me offerings."*[24]

The Patriarchal Mandate Continued

We have seen that after the Flood, the mandate to guard the purity of the messianic bloodline and pass on the ways of the Lord went to Shem. Then out of all his children, it passed to his son Eber (from whose name we get the word Hebrew), then to Abraham, Isaac and Jacob. From there God gave the mandate to the heads of the Twelve Tribes of Israel, then to Moses the Lawgiver. Once Moses wrote down the Law [Torah], the Word of God began to spread more easily.

The Word says, *"Thou hast exalted above everything thy Name [shem] and thy Word."* (Psalms 138:2) He wants us to know Him, and pass down His ways!

Many Patriarchs Lived During The Same Time Period

Notice that the lives of Shem and Eber were very close together in the timeline. What I want you to see is that Abraham and Isaac were very much alive and well during their time on earth. In fact, when Abraham died, both Shem and Eber were still alive!

Abraham's Life Was Threatened Several Times

Abraham was very important to our understanding of the Lord today, so many centuries later. Very little is written in the Bible about his early life. However, according to The Book of Jasher [referenced in Joshua 10:13; 2 Samuel 1:18; and 2 Timothy 3:8], when Abraham was born, there were signs in the heavens foretelling his greatness and promising that his seed would destroy the seed of wickedness on the earth at that time.

Noah and Shem Mentor Abraham

Because of a threat against Abraham's life, his father, Terah, hid his infant son in a cave, where he remained for ten (10) years. When it was safe to leave the cave, Abraham was sent to live with Noah and Shem for thirty-nine (39) years to learn God's ways! It's amazing how little we know of his sacrifice, and of God's heart to make sure Abraham's seed would remain pure and undefiled. Later on in Abraham's life, his enemies tried to kill him again…and he again sought safety with Noah for one month.[25]

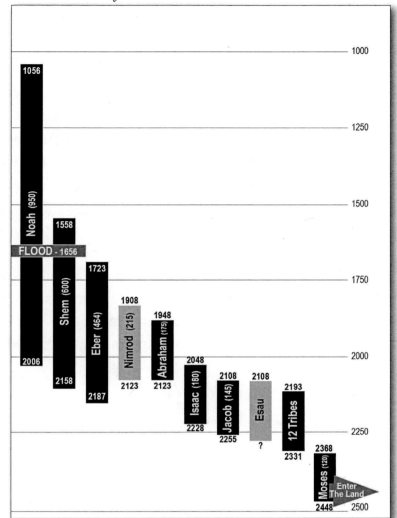

Shem and Eber Mentor Isaac

When Isaac was grown, right after the death of his mother, Sarah, Abraham sent him away to the house of Shem and Eber, to learn the ways of the Lord. Isaac lived with them for three (3) years.[26]

Abraham Mentors Jacob

Isaac was sixty when Rebecca bore his twin sons, Jacob and Esau. The Scriptures do not provide a full biographical profile of these patriarchs, but here are some things worth noting. Many of us tend to view Jacob in his early years as always deceitful. Jasher paints with a larger brush. He writes, *"The boys grew up to their fifteenth year, and they came amongst the society of men. Esau was a designing and deceitful man, and an expert hunter in the field, and Jacob was a man perfect and wise, dwelling in tents, feeding flocks and learning the instructions of the Lord and the commands of his father and mother."[27]* Yes, Jacob was deceitful on occasion, but the historical record shows that he genuinely desired to follow the Lord.

Before Abraham's death, he instructed his son Isaac to *"teach thou thy children and thy seed the instructions of the Lord and his commandments, and teach them the upright way in which they should go, in order that it may be well with them forever. And Isaac answered his father and said unto him, 'That which my Lord has commanded that will I do, and I will not depart from the commands of the Lord my God, I will keep all that he commanded me;' and Abraham blessed his son Isaac, and also his children; and <u>Abraham taught Jacob the instruction of the Lord and his ways</u>."* [28] [Emphasis mine]

Take note of what was happening here: before his death, Abraham taught <u>Jacob</u> the ways of the Lord, not Esau. From the beginning, Jacob was the one who demonstrated a shepherd's heart. He preferred to dwell in the tents and learn from his mother and father, rather than live out in the field hunting as Esau preferred.

Shem and Eber Mentor Jacob

In later years, tensions arose between Jacob and Esau. First, there was the matter of Esau selling his birthright. Rebecca overheard Esau threaten to kill Jacob, our spiritual forefather. Jasher records:

> *"At that time Isaac sent his younger son Jacob to the house of Shem and Eber, and he learned the instructions of the Lord, and Jacob remained in the house of Shem and Eber for thirty-two (32) years, and Esau his brother did not go, for he was not willing to, and he remained in his father's house in the land of Canaan."* [29]

Jacob was with Shem and Eber from age eighteen until he was fifty, which was when he married Rebecca. Notice that Esau had the opportunity to go, but *"he was not willing."* He had no desire to learn the ways of the Lord.

After Jacob's deceit in pretending to be Esau and taking away the blessing of the first-born, Jasher records,

> *"Esau knew that his brother Jacob had done this, and the anger of Esau was kindled against his brother Jacob that he had acted thus toward him…Esau said, 'Is he*

not rightly called Jacob? For he has supplanted me twice, he took away my birthright and now he has taken away my blessing; and Esau wept greatly…and Esau hated his brother Jacob…Jacob was very much afraid of his brother Esau, and he rose up and fled to the house of Eber the son of Shem, and he concealed himself there…fourteen (14) years…and continued to learn the ways of the Lord and his commandments." [30]

God always provides more to those who seek to know Him and His ways, even if they are not perfect. But they have to make sacrifices. First Abraham sacrificed forty-nine (49) years (ten in a cave, and thirty-nine with Noah and Shem), and all told, Jacob spent forty-six (46) years with the Patriarchs learning the ways of God!

What strikes me is how important it was to God that our forefathers pull away from the world and immerse themselves in God's ways. That kind of dedication was critical, especially when you consider that twelve tribes of Israel would come from this one man, Jacob. From his loins would come forth the entire Hebrew nation which was entrusted to teach God's ways to an entire world, and prepare us for the Messiah who would come.

God Still Looks For Seekers Today

God has not changed, has He, Aleeyah? He still looks for those who seek Him with their whole hearts and who want more of Him. The Word says, *"The eyes of the Lord run to and fro throughout the whole earth, to show his might in behalf of those whose heart is blameless toward him."* (2 Chronicles 16:9) The problem is that due to the multiplication of wickedness that Jesus said would come in the Last Days, fewer and fewer people truly want to know the Lord. That would require they pull away from cell phones, texting, TV, Internet and Facebook, and most will simply not do that. God has not changed. He still calls out to His remnant, while the enemy works nonstop to mute His voice through distractions.

"Many are called…but few are chosen." (Matthew 22:16) *Few* in the Greek, *oligos*, means "puny in number." It's as if God planted an entire vineyard, but only a handful of grapes wind up in the remnant. Such is the reality; and yes, there is heartache that more people do not hunger for Him as you and I do.

After walking with the Lord for forty-three years, I see that He carefully guards deeper truths. *"The secret things belong to the Lord."* (Deuteronomy 29:29) He reveals these secrets to His servants the prophets. (Amos 3:7) These are not given to just anyone...but only to those chosen and foreknown, whom He trusts to pass down to others.

Aleeyah, that's why I have resonated so much with your plea for help: the Lord showed you to me, and I heard the cries coming from your heart. You are one who seeks more of Him. My prayer is that He will use me to walk alongside and encourage you in your journey.

In closing this chapter, I want to draw your attention to something our Lord said concerning modern-day scribes – those called to pass down the faith of one generation to another. After a period of teaching by many parables, Jesus explained to His disciples, *"Every scribe who has been <u>trained</u> for the kingdom of heaven is like a <u>householder</u> who brings out of his <u>treasure</u> what is <u>new</u> and what is <u>old</u>."* (Matthew 13:52) [Emphasis mine]

Here's what the underlined words mean.

His Call To Scribes Today

"A true **<u>scribe</u>** *(one with a gift of laying out in words the precepts and truths of God in language others of a particular generation can understand)* who has been **<u>trained</u>** for the kingdom of heaven *(another translation says "one who is <u>converted</u> to the kingdom of heaven," or one preparing others for the kingdom)* is like a **<u>householder</u>** *(one who is entrusted with everything and everyone in that house)* who brings out of his **<u>treasure</u>** *(the real wealth of God's wisdom and understanding revealed to him or her, not silver and gold)* what is **<u>new</u>** *(the Aramaic word used means new as in "fresh" rather than to "age")* and what is **<u>old</u>** *(these are secrets and hidden treasures of antiquity...truths the Lord keeps hidden until a generation or a people arise who hunger for more of Him...at which point He downloads revelation that explains His ways)."*

Aleeyah, it is highly likely that God is calling you as a scribe, just as He has called me. You have a heart for your children, the next generation. I believe He desires to pour such revelation into you that your words will become springs of life to those children who are seeking. The difficulty, especially for us women, is to feed those who are hungry, and let go of those who are going the way of the world. At some point in time, we must realize that just as Jesus spoke regarding the poor, He refers to the lost as if to say: *"The lost you will always have with you."* We must have critical discernment in this day to know where our energies need to be focused.

SUGGESTED PRAYER

"Heavenly Father, I am awed by the dedication of my forefathers to learn the ways of the Lord and pass them down to the next generations. Thank You for their sacrifice. I ask that You give me an increased hunger for Your Word. Make me a true servant of the Lord Jesus and a steward of the mysteries of God. I desire nothing more than to hear from You. If you are calling me to be a scribe, to put in writing the ways of the Lord and communicate them to my generation, I ask that You quicken my mind to write clearly and to accurately portray the majesty that is due Your Name. Every gift You have given me I present to You, to be used in accordance with Your will, for Your glory. In Jesus' name, amen."

LETTER 6
Our Deadliest Battlegrounds

Dear Aleeyah,

Since the Fall, the enemy has been at work primarily on two battlegrounds. His target: every race of people, but most especially those who carry the greatest anointing. These conflicts have been ongoing, throughout history, but as we approach these final days, they are becoming more intense and their casualties even more evident. Because I believe your children carry such an anointing for these Last Days, I see a particularly evil onslaught aimed at your children.

According to my research, here are the battlegrounds. They are intertwined.

I. BATTLE OF THE SEED

From the beginning of time, there have been threats against the messianic line, beginning with Cain and the spilling of Abel's innocent blood. Leaders have come and gone whose agenda was to destroy the Jews: Nebuchadnezzer, Herod, Hitler, Osama bin Laden, and current leaders of almost every country in the Middle East. Thus, their primary goal is to annihilate God's chosen people.

However, if the enemy cannot destroy the godly line, his alternative strategy is to defile or pollute it. It is this strategy we are witnessing now.

Biblically, this pollution first appeared in Genesis 6 with the demonically-tainted race known as the Nephilim. This was Satan's attempt to taint the divine DNA of the children of God and thereby prevent a holy Messiah from ever being born.

How Did The Fallen Angels Corrupt Mankind?

Enoch, our seventh godly patriarch after Adam, wrote in depth how this corruption of humanity took place. It is important for us to understand how the moral compass of mankind got off course.

200 Fallen Angels Came To Earth

"And it came to pass when the children of men had multiplied that in those days were born to them beautiful and fair daughters. And the angels, the sons of heaven, saw and lusted after them, and said to one another: 'Come, let us choose us wives from among the children of men and have children with them.' And Semjaza, who was their leader, said to them: 'I fear you will not agree to do this deed, and I alone shall have to pay the penalty of this great sin.' And they all answered him and said: 'Let us all swear an oath, and all bind ourselves by mutual curses so we will not abandon this plan but to do this thing.' Then they all swore together and bound themselves by mutual curses. And they were in all two hundred who descended in the days of Jared in the summit of Mount Hermon."[31]

This battleground was very much tied to this second one.

II. BATTLE OF KNOWLEDGE OF GOOD AND EVIL

Enoch writes in detail how the early civilization of mankind destroyed itself by being seduced by secret knowledge.

Corruption of All Creation

"And all of them together went and took wives for themselves…and they began to go in to them and to defile themselves with sex with them. And the angels taught them charms and spells, and the cutting of roots, and made them acquainted with plants. And the women became pregnant, and they bare large giants, whose height was three thousand cubits. The giants consumed all the work and toil of men. And when men could no longer sustain them, the giants turned against them and devoured mankind. And they began to sin against birds, and beasts, and reptiles, and fish, and to devour one another's flesh, and drank the blood. Then the earth laid accusation against the lawless ones." [32] [Emphasis mine]

Forbidden Knowledge

"And Azazel (one of the Fallen Angels) *taught men to make swords, and knives, and shields, and breastplates, and taught them about metals of the earth and the art of working them, and bracelets, and ornaments, and the use of antimony* [the use of metals, sulfides, toxins from the earth]*, and the beautifying of the eyelids, and all kinds of precious stones, and all coloring and dyes. And there was great impiety, they turned away from God, and committed fornication, and they were led astray, and became corrupt in all their ways.* (Various Fallen Ones) *taught the casting of spells, and root-cuttings, counter-spells, astrology, portents in the constellations, knowledge of the clouds, the signs of the earth, the signs of the sun, the course of the moon. And as men perished, they cried, and their cry went up to heaven..."*[33]

The Origin of Evil Spirits

In Chapter 15, Enoch explains the origin of evil spirits.

"And now, the giants, who are produced from the spirits and flesh, shall be called evil spirits on the earth, and shall live on the earth. Evil spirits have come out from their bodies because they are born from men and from the holy Watchers, their beginning is of primal origin; They shall be evil spirits on earth, and evil spirits shall they be called spirits of the evil ones. [As for the spirits of heaven, in heaven shall be their dwelling, but as for the spirits of the earth which were born on the earth, on the earth shall be their dwelling.] And the spirits of the giants afflict, oppress, destroy, attack, war, and cause trouble on the earth...and these spirits shall rise up against the children of men and against the women, because they have proceeded from them in the days of the slaughter and destruction."[34] [Emphasis mine]

These passages from Enoch make certain Scriptures come alive with new meaning: Jude 1, Matthew 8 and Jesus casting out spirits from the demoniacs in the country of the Gadarenes. Evil spirits are what resulted when the Nephilim died. When the physical bodies of the Nephilim died, their spirits lived on, earthbound. Even today they wander the earth until the final judgment, looking for someone to inhabit and thereby manifest their fruits of iniquity. We must be wise and learn to spot these manifestations, and cleanse our families from all ungodly soul ties our ancestors had with these familiar spirits.

Aleeyah, take special note that these evil spirits *"shall rise up against the women, because they have proceeded from them…"* In Genesis 3:15, the Lord said to the serpent, *"I will put enmity between you and the woman."* I think that verse means more than just the enmity between the evil one and Messiah [the seed of the woman]. I personally believe it could refer back to Enoch 15 where evil spirits rise up against women, since women were blamed for luring the Watchers and giving birth to the Nephilim, only to have their evil spirits forced to roam the earth following their physical deaths.

In my book *The Levitical Calling,* one of the chapters is *The Levitical Call To Women.* I believe one reason for this enmity is that the enemy knows there is power in a woman's prayers…more specifically, a mother's prayers for her children. The warrior comes out in women – and I might add, Aleeyah – especially in black women! I have experienced firsthand the power of prayers from my sisters of color. I believe this is why God is calling so many women to be intercessors, for we are in the thick of spiritual warfare, which will intensify as we draw closer to the final act.

The Origin Of Music & Fashion To Seduce Children of God

This section is so critical to what is happening with today's young people, I have devoted a separate chapter to it. (See Chapter 7)

The ongoing enticement of mankind today is to **taste** (or "experience") *"the knowledge of good and evil."* There is tremendous seduction in this area. "Come on…everybody's doing it!" is as old as time; however, this is far from a mere "secular influence." On the contrary, these forces are demonic, with webs of such strength that millions are falling like flies, unable to escape its bondage.

Though this enticement affects all areas of our culture, I see it manifested most prominently in the Entertainment and Government sectors…two of the biggest power trips around. Wannabes in both sectors lust for fame, power and money…but to get to that next level, their integrity is always targeted for compromise. How is it compromised? Through *hidden knowledge.*

It's all about those "connections." The promise is this: *"I can get you to that next level, but there is a price to pay for the 'knowledge'* [know-how] *of how the industry works and what you have to do to be in it."* Those who play the game seem to get there…while those who do not are either ridiculed, or stuck on the D-List of notoriety.

The enemy's game is subtle…and it targets many of your children, especially ones gifted in the arts. Aleeyah, the reason your children are being targeted is because there is such giftedness and anointing for them in this industry. I saw it back in the mid-80's, and have dedicated over 25 years to bring the giftedness of African-Americans to the forefront.

People of color are uniquely gifted with incredible expressive talents, but this battlefield is filled with land mines. I have battled it myself, and witnessed much bloodshed. In the last several years, I have seen evidence whereby some of today's most well-known entertainers have made blood oaths and covenants, verbally sacrificing members of their families on the altar of Satan – in exchange for glory and success in the music industry… an industry which is Lucifer's to give.

Nephilim Did Not Die Out With The Flood

Many are shocked by this revelation, but there is much historical and biblical evidence to support this view. The verse that allows the reoccurrence of Nephilim is a simple three-word phrase that most of us gloss over: *"The Nephilim were on the earth in those days, **and also afterward**, when the sons of God came in to the daughters of men, and they bore children to them. These were the mighty men that were of old, the men of renown."* (Genesis 6:4)[Emphasis mine]

Randy DeMain, in his book <u>The Nephilim Agenda</u>, explores the agenda of the fallen Watcher Angels after the Flood. All they were waiting for was an open door to commit the same iniquity as before. As long as Noah's descendants worshipped the Lord and followed His ways, these evil perpetrators could not achieve their mission. In time, however, the children of God began to go their own way and follow the lusts of the flesh. Once these evil angels saw open doors of sexual perversion and idol worship, they were able to re-populate the earth with their demon seed once again.

Nephilim After The Flood

When the twelve spies went to spy out the Promised Land, what did they report seeing? What frightened them so much they wanted to go back to Egypt? Giants…Nephilim!

These giants were superhuman, like Goliath of Gath and Og, King of Bashan…*giants* who terrorized Israel. These weren't just tall men…they were Nephilim.

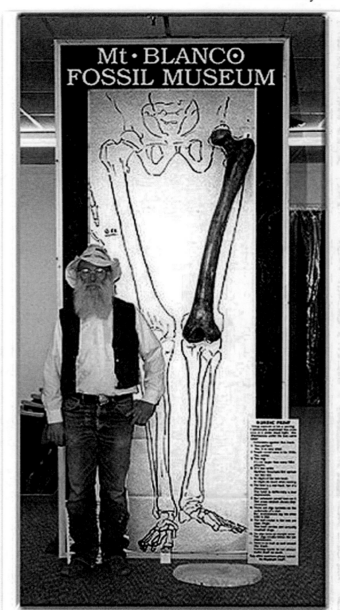

47 inch Human Femur

In the late 1950s, during road construction in south-east Turkey in the Euphrates Valley, many tombs containing the remains of Giants were uncovered. At two sites the leg bones were measured to be about 120 cms "47.24 inches". Joe Taylor, Director of the Mt. BLANCO FOSSIL MUSEUM in Crosbyton, Texas, was commissioned to sculpt this anatomically correct, and to scale, human femur. This "Giant" stood some 14-16 feet tall, and had 20-22 inch long feet. His or Her finger tips, with arms to their sides, would be about 6 feet above the ground. The Biblical record, in Deuteronomy 3:11 states that the Iron Bed of Og, King of Bashan was 9 cubits by 4 cubits or approximately 14 feet long by 6 feet wide!

GENESIS 6:4
There were Nephilim (Giants) in the earth in those days; and also after that when the sons of God (Angels?) came in unto the daughters of men, and they bare children to them, the same became mighty men which were of old, men of renown.

More Info & Replicas available at mtblanco1@aol.com or www.mtblanco.com
Mt. Blanco Fossil Museum • P.O. Box 559, Crosbyton, TX 79322 • 1-800-367-7454

Archeological Evidence
Check out this fossil discovery in Turkey's Euphrates Valley in the 1950's. [35]

DeMain writes,

"The angels did not waste any time after the flood. They went back to work trying to spoil the line of Adam. God in His wisdom knew this and separated the offspring by their looks and gave them, no doubt, a warring nature, one that would be their downfall. It would be true to say we have not seen or heard of any recently, but that is not to say God has stopped them; it might merely be the plan of Lucifer to bide his time. Who knows, though, maybe these alien creatures we are told exist are another form of angelic children. It is true to say during biblical times they existed, but Scripture uses other names to describe these degraded fallen angels and their descendants after the flood, in addition to the word Nephilim. [36]

They are:
- Anakim – descendants of Nephilim. (Numbers 13:33)
- Emim – the proud deserters, terrors, race of giants. (Genesis 14:5; Deuteronomy 2:11)
- Zamzummims – the evil plotters. (Deuteronomy 2:20)
- Zuphim – watchers, angels who descended, distinct from 'holy watchers' aligned with God. (Numbers 23)
- Sepharim – "the many…"
- Zuzim – the evil ones, roaming things. (Genesis 14:5)
- Rephaim – from the root *rapha* that means *spirits, shades*. (Genesis 14:5) [37]

In Deuteronomy 3:11 we read, *"Only Og the king of Bashan was left of the remnant of the Rephaim."* *Remnant* in Hebrew means the "residue" or "remainder" of the Rephaim race of giants. Thus, the biblical record indicates that due to the many wars between them and the Israelites, the Lord allowed the giants to die out slowly. Can they, or will they return?

DeMain offers this insight,

"As we can see, they [giants] were in abundance but God slowly destroyed them and gave most of their land to Israel. However, I am sure they will return when the time is right. Who knows…maybe the antichrist will come from the line of the fallen angels." [38]

Where Are These Beings Now?

When God heard the cries of torment coming from the earth, Enoch recorded His judgment against the Fallen Watchers:

> *"And the Lord said to Michael: 'Go, bind Semjaza and his team who have associated with women and have defiled themselves in their uncleanness. When their sons have slain one another, and they have seen the destruction of their beloved ones, <u>bind them fast for seventy generations</u> under the hills of the earth, until the day of the consummation of their judgment and until the eternal judgment is accomplished."*[39]
> [Emphasis mine]

Please note, Aleeyah, that the Apostle John wrote in the book of the Revelation of Jesus Christ that these fallen angels who were bound **will** be released, if they are not already.

> *"The fifth angel blew his trumpet, and I saw a star fallen from heaven to earth, and he was given the key of the shaft of the bottomless pit; he opened the shaft of the bottomless pit, and from the shaft rose smoke like the smoke of a great furnace, and the sun and the air were darkened with the smoke from the shaft. Then from the smoke came locusts on the earth...they have as king over them the angel of the bottomless pit; his name in Hebrew is Abaddon, and in Greek he is called Apollyon."*
> (Revelation 9:1-11) [Emphasis mine]

Look at these photos on the next page from the past two decades. I cannot say for certain that this bottomless pit has been opened; but if not, then I believe that something similar will occur where these powerful demonic principalities will come spewing forth into the earth realm.

Eruptions In The Earth

2010 BP Oil Spill In Gulf of Mexico
Source: AP Photo/US Coast Guard, File

Mount St. Helens May 18, 1980: Before eruption (above)... *the eruption itself* (right)
Source: U.S. Geological Survey Photographic Library. Photos by Austin Post. (http://libraryphoto.cr.usgs.gov)

8.9 Magnitude Earthquake Triggers
13-Ft. Tsunami On Japan's Eastern Coast
March 11, 2011
Source: AP Photo/Kyodo News

LETTER 7
The Origin Of Music & Fashion

Dear Aleeyah,

Music is important to most cultures, but seems especially so to people of color...simply because music is a vital part of your collective soul and one of your greatest gifts. It is also an arena of tremendous temptation.

As a composer, I am especially sensitive to sound, and how the enemy can corrupt it. In the last several years, the Lord has given me much revelation on what happens when "praise music" is performed by musicians, singers and dancers who are living immoral lives. (See Chapter 9, *"The Nature of Defilement"* and Chapter 10, *"The Sexual Assault On The Church"*)

The Origin Of Music

We know from Ezekiel 28 and Isaiah 14 something of the musical giftedness and calling of Lucifer. His assigned place was to hover over the very throne of God.

> *"With an anointed guardian cherub I placed you; you were on the holy mountain of God; in the midst of the stones of fire you walked, You were blameless in your ways from the day you were created, till iniquity was found in you...your heart was proud because of your beauty; you corrupted your wisdom for the sake of your splendor...By the multitude of your iniquities, <u>in the unrighteousness of your trade</u> you profaned your sanctuaries..."* (Ezekiel 28:14-17) [Emphasis mine]

What God is saying here is that the <u>way</u> Lucifer conducted his "trade" or "professional calling" of leading worship and praise among God's created spiritual beings was *unrighteous*. This is what is happening today in many churches!

In some translations, this passage reads that *tabrets* (tambourines) and *pipes* were a part of Lucifer…not something he played…rather, they were part of his being. Music poured out of him. It's who he is; and throughout history, Lucifer has been **the** gatekeeper to "making it in the music industry," and even more important to God, "making it in the **gospel** music business." Hear me, I am not saying that everyone who is successful in either music industry sector has sold out to Satan. What I am saying is that everyone who attempts to "make it" *there* will be faced with incredibly powerful temptations to compromise their integrity. The majority, I am convinced, will lose. The temptations to immorality are that great, especially in this evil day where wickedness is multiplying.

The Allure Of Glitz & Know-How

Lucifer was covered with precious stones, and Ezekiel 28:12 says he was *"the signet of perfection, full of wisdom and perfect in beauty"* – in other words, the fullest measure of wisdom and knowledge that Jehovah gave to any of His created beings was given to *"the god of this world."* Lucifer knew everything the Almighty made possible to know! That's why the music industry is so seductive. Fame-seekers will sell out to anyone who promises them the "know-how" to get to the top. This knowledge is invaluable, and the level of giftedness given to musicians who sell out is enviable. That's the lure, and the not-so-subtle dance of industry seduction. Lucifer is the gatekeeper.

The Originator of Praise Music

Lucifer's job was to lead all creation in singing songs of praise to the Almighty. He was the worship leader of all worship leaders…until he desired the praise and glory for himself rather than God. Ever since Lucifer fell and God cast him out of heaven, the Almighty has been searching throughout the earth to find sounds of pure praise to lead His angelic and earthly creation…for it is praise wherein He has chosen to be enthroned. (Psalms 22:3)

Aleeyah, my heart is heavy with sorrow seeing so many sell out the purity of their worship for the renown that is as old as time. I know you grieve this as well. From my vantage point – as a 40-year survivor of the entertainment industry – this seduction is especially targeting the black gospel music sector.

Modern-day Levites are given the divine mandate to guard the purity of the altar. How sad the Lord must be when churches permit preachers, musicians, worship leaders, singers and dancers [all participants at the altars] to live immoral lives. When Satan perverts those who "broadcast sound waves," their words and music are layered with immorality. Many of today's churches might as well spew literal filth all over those sitting in the pews. I believe this is why we are witnessing such an explosion of homosexuality, adultery, pornography, pedophilia, addictions, incest, abortions and illegitimacy.

Sound Waves Can Be Corrupted

Music [sound waves produced by singing or playing, strumming, hitting or blowing an instrument] has a supernatural power to penetrate a person's spirit. That's why King Saul was delivered from demonic oppression when David played the harp...how a patriotic band can inspire troops to risk their lives for their country...why heavy metal music can inflame a listener's passions to commit murder...how a rap song can inspire gang warfare and rape...or why a soft ballad can seduce a listener to cross over marital boundaries into an adulterous affair.

A musical note and a single lyric are, in and of themselves, harmless. However, the thing that has the power to go into another's spirit is the *heart* of the writer and performer. Jesus said, *"What comes out of the mouth proceeds from the heart, and this defiles a man. For out of the heart come evil thoughts, murder, adultery, fornication, theft, false witness, slander."* (Matthew 15:18-19)

Think about it: a good number of megachurches spend a lot of money hiring the best musicians for their worship services, reasoning that the people come to hear good music. Gone, then, are the levitical gatekeepers known as Gershonites whose mandate is to guard the purity of the altar and protect it from any and all defilement.

Before ministering in sacrificial offerings, our levitical forefathers had to undergo numerous baths and rituals <u>one week prior</u> to their assigned time of ministry. It was critical that their hearts and bodies were clean. If not, a holy God would strike them dead. God gave us in the Old Testament an important *tavneet* or "Picture" of the importance of levitical cleansing before ministering at the altar.

Depiction of the inner chamber of the Temple where levitical priests were ritually cleansed. (Artist: D'Ann Medlin. Used by permission.)

Who are the gatekeepers of righteousness today?

Where are those who can discern that the keyboard player is carrying on with one of the dancers? Or that the minister has a woman on the side? This should never be allowed in the Church. A true Levite should know by the Spirit everything about those who minister at the altar, and insist that those who defile themselves by immoral behavior sit down and refrain from playing, singing or preaching until which time as they are restored. That is the true levitical mandate for those who minister in churches.

What Happens When This Is Not Done?

The *immoral heart* of a minister "attaches itself to" or "corrupts" the sound waves that he or she broadcasts into the air. If it is music, then it pierces a listener's soul and defiles it. I have spent several years researching ELFs (Extra Low Frequency) sound waves. With just one click on Google you will find that the U.S. Navy has spent more than $16 million conducting scientific research into the effects of low frequency underwater sound on humans and animals. It also revealed research conducted at the University of Gothenburg, in Sweden: *"In nature, frequencies below 200Hz are signals of thunder, volcano eruptions, earthquakes or storms - events that are likely to induce arousal or fear."* [38]

The technology surrounding "Manchurian Candidate" assassins is not fiction. It is based on scientific research. Low frequency sound waves of verbal suggestions can make assassins kill "on command" and inflame riots. This technology has existed since the 80's, and has been perfected by many scientists and nations, among them Russia and the U.S.

It is this same strategy the enemy uses in our churches. He is sliming innocent congregations every single week by ministers, musicians, singers and dancers who think they are covering up their sin. They are not. *"God is not mocked...whatever a man sows, that he will also reap."* (Galatians 6:7)

I believe that today's churches are one of the central breeding grounds for all manner of immorality...because this strategy is being used and appears to be working well: **Slime the people and keep God away from the Church, knowing full well He cannot abide where there is moral defilement.**

How Satan First Inhabited Music

I want to share with you the oral and written tradition of how music was first used to lure the children of God to their own destruction, especially targeting leaders who demonstrated charisma and power.

> *"After Cain had gone down to the land of dark soil, and his children had multiplied therein, there was one of them, whose name was Genun, son of Lamech the blind who slew Cain. But as to this Genun* [translated Jubal in most Bible translations]*, Satan came into him in his childhood; and he made sundry trumpets and horns, and string instruments, cymbals and psalteries, and lyres and harps, and flutes; and he played on them at all times and at every hour. And <u>when he played on them, Satan came into them,</u> so that from among them were heard beautiful and sweet sounds, that ravished the heart. Then he gathered companies upon companies to play on them; and when they played, it pleased well the children of Cain, who inflamed themselves with sin among themselves, and burnt as with fire; while Satan inflamed their hearts, one with another, and increased lust among them."*[40] [Emphasis mine]

He Taught How To Make Alcohol

> *"Satan also taught Genun to bring strong drink out of corn…thus did this Genun multiply sin exceedingly; he also acted with pride, and taught the children of Cain to commit all manner of the grossest wickedness, which they knew not. <u>Then Satan, when he saw that they yielded to Genun and hearkened to him in every thing he told them, rejoiced greatly,</u> increased Genun's understanding, until he took iron and with it made weapons of war. Then when they were drunk, hatred and murder increased among them; one man used violence against another to teach him evil taking his children and defiling them before him. And when men saw they were overcome, and saw others that were not overpowered, those who were beaten came to Genun, took refuge with him, and he made them his confederates. Then sin increased among them greatly; until a man married his own sister, or daughter, or mother…so that there was no more distinction of relationship, and they no longer knew what is iniquity…; and they angered God the Judge, who had created them."* [41]

How The Children of God Were Enticed

The evildoers were no longer content to do evil by themselves. The next step was to entice the godly.

> *"Genun gathered together companies that played on horns and on all the other instruments at the foot of the Holy Mountain; and <u>they did so in order that the children of Seth who were on the Holy Mountain should hear it</u>. But when the children of Seth heard the noise, they wondered, and came by companies, and stood on the top of the mountain to look at those below; and they did thus a whole year…<u>When Genun saw that they were being won over to him little by little, Satan entered into him,</u> and taught him to make dyeing-stuffs for garments of divers patterns, and made him understand how to dye crimson and purple…and the sons of Cain who wrought all this, and shone in beauty and gorgeous apparel, gathered together at the foot of the mountain in splendour, with horns and gorgeous dresses, and horse races, committing all manner of abominations. Meanwhile the children of Seth, who were on the Holy Mountain, prayed and praised God, in the place of the hosts of angels who had fallen…but <u>they relaxed from their fasting and praying, and from the counsel of Jared their father</u>."* [42] [Emphasis mine]

Everything described above is happening today. As believers, we are compromised when we ignore the time required to heed the spiritual disciplines of fasting and praying. We wrestle with such distraction that most of us have difficulty thinking straight, much less spending time alone with God. I can well understand the motivations of the Quakers, Puritans and Amish who felt so encroached upon by the evil in the world that they pulled away from society altogether. I must admit there are times when I consider moving to some secluded place in the mountains, to devote more time to the Lord.

The irony, Aleeyah, is that though music has been a great source of temptation for many of your children, it is one of your greatest strengths.

People of Color Are Anointed For Music

The year this book was inspired [2009], I was asked to head up a creative research project for an international record label. Non-disclosure agreements prevent me from discussing the particulars, but what I can share involves research into our country's early history of gospel music.

Because of my interest in Black Gospel, I found myself reading about the slave era and how music began to be exported all over the world.

Gospel Music was born on plantations, amidst the tremendous heartache your people suffered. Fearful of uprisings, many American slave owners did not allow blacks to use traditional African instruments, nor were they allowed to play or sing their native songs. But God had infused music deep within the collective soul of His people of color. It could not be contained. Blues, Jazz, Negro Spirituals, Ragtime and Call & Response Gospel Music were born. These are uniquely African-American musical styles and have influenced all of American culture. Before long, interest mounted from across the seas from whence the slaves had come in the first place!

Germany was the first country where gospel music first expanded into Europe. This country of "stiff, somber Germans" now boasts a long tradition of church choirs, especially in cities and towns with American military bases where there is a vibrant black community. Gospel concerts are very popular in Germany. According to GospelFlava. com, *"People are attracted by the heavenly sound of the voices and the irresistible rhythms of today's gospel music. This is especially so in the former East Germany where, after 40 years of socialism, only a small segment of the population is Christian."*

The Lord desires to bless such musical expressions of praise and worship. He desires to touch people all over the world. I see this as a huge calling for many of your people with musical performing gifts. The global impact will be huge <u>if</u> these sounds of praise come from righteous worshippers.

Ironically, the young high school student who originally inspired my black musical in the mid-80's now heads up an annual gospel workshop in Germany where she is based.[43]

In South Africa, Gospel Music has become one of the country's top-selling genres. South Africa is a nation of strong religious faith, but leaders fear that many artists record for the money more than the ministry. We need to be especially careful that we do not export gifted musicians with impure motives, for we will be held responsible for how we use music to influence others for the Kingdom of God.

The Jewish People Await Pure Sounds of Praise

Several years ago, so the story goes, Barbra Streisand was so moved by a spiritual sung by gifted African-American opera singer Jessye Norman that she recorded a gospel CD of her own: *Higher Ground.* It is one of my favorites. Norman's performance inspired Streisand [a Jew] to explore her own spiritual roots. I see this story as a microcosm of what is to come.

What I see prophetically is that to the degree your children's praise is pure will be the degree that the veil of blindness will be lifted from the eyes of the Jewish people. In that glorious day, they will receive their Messiah…and the full remnant of the children of God [from Shem, Japheth and Ham] will join together in glorious worship and service to the King.

It is the pure voices of His people of color that the world is waiting for. Your people have been uniquely gifted for such a time as this.

SUGGESTED PRAYER
"Holy Father, I ask that You protect me and my children from music that is corrupted by defiling spirits. I ask that the music that flows from my heart be filled with pure sounds of praise, befitting the King. Increase my discernment and help me to do all that I can to guard the purity of the altars in the churches where I am involved. I pray for Your mercy to overtake my children and grandchildren and deliver them from the evils of this wicked generation. Keep us from falling, Lord. May we be preserved blameless before the presence of Your glory with rejoicing. To the only God, our Savior through Jesus Christ my Lord, be glory, majesty, dominion, and authority, before all time and now and forever. Amen. (Jude 24-25)

LETTER 8
Paying The Price For Giftedness

Dear Aleeyah,

When I consider people of color, one word immediately comes to mind: *gifted*. Gifted in music...gifted in the performing arts...gifted in sports...gifted in strength – the kind of giftedness that garners attention and acclaim. Unfortunately, these gifted ones are targeted by the enemy for destruction. Though many of the stories I relate in this chapter deal with the music industry, the application for those in the sports or other spotlight careers is just as true.

I remember sitting around a lunch table listening to one of my spiritual mentors, Barbara Wentroble, Founder of International Breakthrough Ministries in Dallas, Texas. She asked everyone to introduce ourselves and say what we hoped to get from this informal time together. She wanted us to get to know one another better, given that we were all part of this apostolic network. Across the table, a young woman stood up, looked straight at Barbara and declared, *"I'm here because I want what you've got!"*

I shuddered, knowing this young woman spoke without realizing the implications of coveting another's level of anointing. A similar thing happened when the mother of James and John asked Jesus if her sons could sit on either side of Him in His Kingdom. He gave a sobering reply, *"You do not know what you are asking. Are you able to drink the cup that I am to drink?"* (Matthew 20:22)

The necessary requirement to walk in Christ-like anointing is to have every ounce of your flesh crucified. As we continue our levitical journey, no matter how long we have been on it, we must understand this principle. To walk in complete fullness of wisdom, knowledge, understanding, might, counsel, reverence, piety, mercy – plus the power to raise people from the dead, cast out demonic spirits, and heal every manner of infirmity requires *total* death to self. This sort of "death" is not pretty. It is painful...leaves visible scars...and is all-too-often public. Yes, to carry the full anointing that God desires to give us...well, let's face it: very few are willing to pay the price.

What Is Giftedness?

There are several well-known passages in Scripture that mention *giftedness*. Proverbs 18:16 says, *"A man's gift makes room for him."* The Hebrew word is *mattan* meaning "a present or reward." It comes from another Hebrew word *nathan*, a root word which means "to give, appoint, ascribe, assign or bestow."

The Apostle Paul exhorts Timothy, *"I remind you to rekindle the gift of God that is within you through the laying on of my hands."* (2 Tim. 1:6) And again, *"Do not neglect the gift you have, which was given you by prophetic utterance when the elders laid their hands upon you."* (I Tim. 4:14) The Greek word for *gift* is *charisma* meaning "a divine gratuity or gift, a spiritual endowment, a miraculous faculty." Gifts like these come directly from the Father to an individual. They are appointed, bestowed, and assigned to a person as a spiritual endowment, capable of working miracles in others when fully yielded and empowered by Holy Spirit.

As one who has been called to the Arts & Entertainment sector for over 40 years, I have seen much giftedness, and witnessed much abuse and misuse of these endowments. Giftedness in music, performing, acting, dancing, etc. especially attract demonic forces whose goal is to seduce the one gifted and prevent the Holy Spirit from being operational within that gift. Remember, music was where the evil one was originally assigned by the Almighty. He was created to be the most anointed worship leader of all. After his fall, precipitated by pride and his own sense of entitlement, he was fueled by an unrelenting desire to destroy those likewise gifted.

How Does Giftedness Grow?

Every divine faculty and gift is given to us to steward. We are exhorted to invest time and money into the development of our gifts...to use them to their fullest potential even if only one person is in the audience...to inwardly and outwardly direct all praise to the One to whom praise belongs...to give of our gift freely with no thought of entitlement...to shun those who would try to steal or manipulate our gifts for ungodly gain. When we properly steward our gifts, they not only grow and strengthen, but other gifts we never had begin to blossom. It is not uncommon, for example, to see someone start out with one gift...and as she begins to use it freely, other gifts arise. The world is full of multi-gifted people. Not all of them are believers...for gifts and callings are assigned and bestowed before we are born. We are each given the same opportunity to learn about our giftedness, inquire about the Giver and ultimately give praise where praise is due.

A Songwriter's Introduction To Giftedness

I have written songs ever since I was 13, and was on the college circuit for years as a one-woman show. I played the piano and guitar, wrote songs, sang, spoke, designed PR materials, produced my album and administrated my bookings. It was the "doing of all those things" wherein I was extremely fulfilled, free to express myself without anyone looking over my shoulder, criticizing or squelching me. I am what some call "multi-gifted." The Lord kept pushing me into areas I didn't know how to do, like doing an entire 30-minute TV show by myself with a week's notice! But as soon as I attained some level of mastery, He would push me into another arena.

In 1977, my sense of calling became more finely-tuned: I had an inner "knowing" that I was to born to be a songwriter. Thus, I began to invest time, money and energies into learning everything I could about the craft of writing songs. I travelled in and out of Nashville...read every songwriting book I could find...formed relationships with publishers and other songwriters to develop my gifting. To be a credible songwriter in Nashville, you need to be able to play multiple instruments, sing, write melodies and lyrics, and record your own demos. In other words, the entry level requirement for being a Nashville songwriter is to be multi-gifted. The harder part followed: enduring snide remarks behind your back, lies told about you to publishers to stop your advancement, stealing a favorite chord progression that you've worked on for months, endless rejections, the hype by a publisher who says, *"This is a monster hit!"* only to find that song still in its case a year later, covered by dust on his shelf.

The music business in and of itself can be insidious...and only the strong survive. If you say, *"Oh, I'm in gospel music...not secular,"* let me assure you that the treachery is just as real.

The Seductive Climb Up The Ladder

I remember when my husband and I moved to Nashville in 1980 so I could dedicate myself to my songwriting pursuit. I had to know if my sense of calling was real or "smoke and mirrors." In my small town of Gainesville, Georgia, I may have been an award-winning songwriter; but in Nashville, I was one among thousands who were big fish in their little ponds, too. I had zero confidence, and no clue how I would fare among the new kids in town. The first weekend, we heard about a songwriting contest at a local club...an open mic event where songwriters sign up, go out and sing, and then the winner was voted on by the crowd. I took my guitar out of its case and with knees shaking, gave it my best shot. Lo and behold, I won the competition! The seduction of applause enticed me to continue to climb up this slippery ladder to the land of "making it." Little did I know it would cost me my family, and leave me financially and emotionally devastated.

I recount the entire journey in my book, *Wired For Creativity*, plus the lessons of over sixty biblical principles the Lord graciously taught me over a 3-year wilderness when I was totally broken.

The Call To The Marketplace

My calling has always been in the secular arena...more specifically, Arts & Entertainment. As difficult as the journey has been, the climb up the ladder is part of the assignment. It's called "paying one's dues," and there are no shortcuts. It is paying the price to gain credibility and learn the language of the "mountain."

Wherever a person's calling – to Marketplace or to Ministry – the same principles apply. Please allow me to share some of my experience with you...to encourage you, and prepare you and your gifted children to deal with what lies ahead.

Lessons For The Journey

- *Watch Out When You Get Singled Out.* While you are in God's training ground in your specific callling, you will likely experience a lot of support. That's because you are no threat to anybody else. The reality is that when you are broken and needy...going to school...living hand-to-mouth trying to make ends meet...oh, you'll get some great prophetic words and people laying hands on you with uplifting prayers. But once the spotlight falls on you and you start pulling ahead of the pack, watch out! It's not a pretty picture. The mood swings suddenly, the fangs come out, and friends you thought you had want nothing to do with you. I did a radio interview with another of my mentors, Elizabeth Hairston-McBurrows, a pioneer in the liturgical dance movement. She told of coming to the Lord in the 70's and faithfully going to church week after week, soaking up everything she could about the Lord. She freely danced in the aisles during worship, unaware of anyone but her and the Lord. She completed every assignment the pastor gave, was always on the front row, and pretty soon he began to single her out. He would call on her in discussion groups, because he knew she would have the answer. He invited her to stand by him and pray for people while he ministered to them, asking what the Lord showed her for the people. He pushed her forward to minister in dance and song and to flow among the people. She became his protegé. To others, she was the "teacher's pet," when all along this man of God simply recognized her gifting and felt led to help develop it.

• *It's Lonely At The Top.* When you begin moving in your giftedness, and your gifts get noticed by others, there will be a parting of the ways with old friends. I remember singing back-up in 1972 at an outdoor concert for 100,000 college students in Dallas, Texas. This was at the height of the Jesus Movement. The singer was Katie Hanley, the Broadway star who played the part of Mary Magdalene in *Jesus Christ Superstar.* That event was a memorable thrill for me. One day after rehearsal, Katie singled me out and invited me to her room the next day for lunch. *"Why me?,"* I thought. *"Surely she must have lots of friends."* There in her plush suite, the waiter brought in our lunch, and Katie and I got to know each other a little. She was very sincere in her faith...a lovely person. But she was extremely lonely. Being a "star," she was unapproachable to most, and said how few people she could really trust, even in Christian circles. In today's church circles, many look at Elizabeth Hairston and long for the level of anointing she carries when she ministers in dance. You must realize that when you reach this level of anointing – or the level of stardom Katie Hanley had – you will lose many "friends" along the way. You will be shunned, talked about, made fun of, lied about, even betrayed. *Why does this happen?* The truth is: your friends no longer feel good about themselves when they are around you. At this juncture, you have a critical choice to make: Do you want to push forward to all God has for you, even if you have to go alone? Or, do you want to stay where you are, settle for mediocrity, hang on to those friends at all cost and never reach your destined place? This is no easy juncture. Listen, you may even lose a spouse along the way...one who is threatened by you. No one ever talks about that possibility. But if it should happen, what would the Lord have you do? Stop growing? Or, continue growing in humility and pray for the one who struggles with low self-esteem? I need to say here that I have witnessed many women asserting themselves out front, almost in defiance of their husband's wishes. The Word of God requires that as women, we are to have a submissive spirit, and one which honors our husbands. I would never advise going against your husband's wishes. I remember speaking with two women who were having this very struggle. They knew they were being called of God to greater consecration, but their husbands were adamantly opposed. One husband yelled, *"Why do we have to spend this money on some stupid dance costume? Why can't we just be like we used to and go to church like normal people?"* There are no easy answers. Such affliction requires periods of prayer and fasting. Ask your spouse for his blessing for you to continue to pursue your calling, and trust the Lord to change his heart. *"Many are called, but few are chosen."* (Matthew 22:14)

• *Others Watch Your Every Move!* When you come into your own, you're so focused on the doors opening before you, you're clueless to who's watching from behind. But don't kid yourself...there are many who watch every move you make. They take note of what conferences you sign up for... who your spiritual mentor is...what idea you are pitching...what books are speaking to you...what your next strategy is. One day, you wake up and realize that so-and-so is actually trying to <u>be</u> you! This has happened to me on more than one occasion. A former "best friend" and business partner tried to steal my biggest agency client for herself and open her own agency. Another time, two entertainment industry partners tried to cut me out of a TV series that I had created, right after a Hollywood producer flew in to meet with us. It stings. In Nashville, a male songwriter I had never seen before verbally cut me down in front of a publisher's executive assistant. I was so humiliated, I ran out of the office as fast as I could...and cried all the way home. I couldn't imagine what I had done to this man. I called one of my mentors, the late hit songwriter, John Jarrard. When I told him what happened and that I was thinking of quitting the business, he laughed and said, *"Don't you dare. That's just what he wants you to do."* He then told me the story of when he first came to Music City and signed on as a writer for Alabama's music publishing company. One day, one of the more mature hit songwriters pulled John aside and said in a very sincere tone, *"Listen man, this gig just ain't for you. You don't have what it takes to really make it and I hate to see you beat yourself up day after day. I think you'd be happier in another line of work."* John had given everything he had to his songwriting pursuits. His diabetes got out of hand when he moved to Nashville...he lost his eyesight completely, and learned to ride the bus and make his way to the publishing company every day guided by a cane. John had what it took to succeed, and later went on to rack up many number one hits...but like me, at that moment, he was devastated...until one older and more experienced told him just what he was telling me. I said, *"But John, I never saw that guy before!"* He said, *"But he saw you...he watched you go in and out of the A & R guys' offices, knowing that they're out there pitching songs to the producers. You were a threat... and because you are young and naive, he thought he could get rid of one more com-petition."* In Christian circles, the same games are played...only much more subtly. There are many watching to see what doors you may open for them. Ask the Lord to protect you and make you aware of what is going on. Your inner compass (Holy Spirit) will alert you when someone has encroached a little too close onto your turf. That's when it is wise to take a few steps back from them...guard your tongue...keep your own counsel...don't talk about everything you're doing. Steal away into God's presence, for He is the only refuge who is completely trustworthy with no self-serving agenda.

- *Focus On Your Gifts, No One Else's.* Paul and Barnabus started out to-gether. The Holy Spirit set them both apart while at Antioch. They were perceived as co-ministers, equally gifted, both highly regarded for their faithfulness and calling from God. While on the first journey, however, Paul's gifts became more evident. His speaking abilities attracted greater crowds. He demonstrated signs and wonders much more than Barnabus did. Paul's leadership gifts pushed him into the spotlight, while Barnabus likely began to feel like chopped liver. Ultimately, the two argued over the direction of their next mission trip...and split up. This isn't a "thus saith the

Lord," but my sense is that Paul did not excel in emotional intelligence. He probably did not pull Barnabus aside and encourage him in his giftedness of discipleship and one-on-one exhortation. He didn't help soothe Barnabus' bruised ego. In like manner, Barnabus likely drew people around him who made him feel better about himself. Perhaps he even became critical of Paul and tried to point out his faults to others. I have been in both positions: one where I was clearly the one favored...and at other times, one who struggled with self-esteem issues watching a friend rise to a higher place of visibility. Both positions are fraught with great emotional affliction. The wisdom is to keep your eyes on pleasing the Lord with your gifts, pray for others around you, and always look for opportunities to encourage them. If they turn on you, shake the dust off your feet and move on. Yes, it will hurt. You'll have scars. But is your goal to stop....or to finish the race? Further study revealed that when Paul and Barnabus split, Barnabus was never heard from again. Don't be disqualified because of a critical, jealous spirit.

• *If You're The One Left Behind.* This is a critical test. God is watching to see if you will genuinely wish your friend well, and rejoice with her...or if you stop growing and set up camp at Grumble Mountain. Ask the Lord to reveal if there is something wrong with your motives or attitudes that are keeping you from progressing, and tell Him that you want more than anything for Him to show you so you can align with your destined place.

• *"Do Nothing Through Strife Or Vainglory."* In Philippians 2:3, Paul writes, *"...in humility let each regard his neighbor better than himself."* Two words need further commentary. The word for *vainglory* is *kenodoxia* which means "empty glorying and self-conceit." I am on the board of an organization which had a worker who puffed herself up to members, as if she were the only qualified person to manage the organization. She was totally out of order because she was "employed" by the organization...not a member of it. This is "empty glorying and self-conceit." Proverbs 27:2 says, *"Let another praise you, and not your own mouth."* We will be judged by God Almighty for every foolish word we utter, especially if those words tear down one whom He has chosen for a particular assignment. The second important word is *strife*, the Greek word being *eritheia* which means "intrigue or faction." People who operate in strife are very gifted in manipulating through words and actions which in turn form factions within a group. These factions are deadly and must be dismantled at all cost, or they will destroy what God is doing with that group. If you are in leadership, it is critical that you stand up to this striving spirit...and like Donald Trump, say, *"You're fired!"*

• *Invest In Your Giftedness.* This is a lesson I learned from my father, and it has been invaluable. While in a challenging Executive MBA program in 2008, I calculated that I have invested a combined total of fifty-seven years and over $6 million in time and money on six different ventures...five of which have to do with my call to the Arts & Entertainment sector. I don't say this to put anyone under the pile nor puff myself up. Rather, this has been part of the price I have been asked to pay for my levitical call. No matter where you are in your journey, ask the Father how <u>He</u> wants you to invest in the gifts He has given you to steward. Think of the Parable of the Talents. Though *talents* is a monetary term, begin to consider your gifts as deposits of wealth placed in you by God. He desires the same qualities of aggressive, faithful stewardship of our giftedness just like He requires of monetary stewards. You will <u>not</u> get to your assigned place without extreme sacrifice...but fear not....the Lord is with you! Don't look at your apparent lack of funds. The miracle of supply always comes in times of lack, not plenty. He is the source of every financial sacrifice you will be called on to make.

• *Above All Else, Guard Your Heart.* There are those who will use you for their own ends and then disregard you when they have gotten what they want. Two helpful principles I have learned for this part of the journey are: (1) <u>Trust very few</u>. *"Jesus did not trust Himself to them."* (John 2:24) Jesus, filled with Holy Spirit 24-7, operated in keen discernment. As you spend time with the Father, He will give you the ability to discern the true motivations in others around you. (2) <u>Detach yourself</u>. When it's all said and done, it is <u>your</u> journey...<u>your</u> life you have to give account for. Jesus said very clearly that unless you renounce all your possessions and everyone in your life, you are not fit to be His disciple. One of the prices you may have to pay is losing someone or something very dear to you. This is not written to frighten you...but to explain that the ones you look up to in ministry have <u>all</u> paid dearly for the anointing they carry. They have spent days, weeks, years before the Lord...on the floor...sitting in silence while the rest of their friends go on about life seemingly without a care. That's because they heard the call and chose to stay the course. Their calling requires everything they have, and whatever level of anointing they walk in came through testing, re-testing and refining by the Father. They kept their eyes on Jesus, not on those who were trying to pull them down to join them in mediocrity. You see, the Father longs to give His children great anointing to minister to others, but understands that few are able to walk in it. The narrow path is strewn with the remains of those who could not – or would not – finish the journey. I pray you are not among them.

SUGGESTED PRAYER

"Lord, You are the Giver of every perfect gift. Help me to understand the many gifts You have given me to steward. Give me the courage to keep to the course, and not listen to those who would try to steer me away from Your plan for my life. Give me the strength and willingness to sacrifice and invest in my gifts, and the ability to always view them with humility...for I desire that You receive my highest praise. Please give me godly mentors and friends who sincerely desire my good and will hold me accountable to walk righteously in my giftedness. Amen."

LETTER 9
The Nature Of Defilement

Dear Aleeyah,

The Hebrew word for *defilement* means "to be foul or contaminated" in a ceremonial or moral sense, or to pollute oneself. The verb tense is in the middle voice that indicates that this is something we do TO ourselves. It is in our power NOT to be defiled.

This is a diagram that depicts how the Levites were to encamp around the Lord's presence in the Tabernacle.

Moses, Aaron and their families encamped on the East of the Tabernacle; the levitical family of Kohathites encamped on the South; the Gershonites on the West; and the Merarites on the North. You can clearly see how the Lord chose and trained the Levites to be a buffer between a holy God and an unclean people. He desires to dwell in our midst.

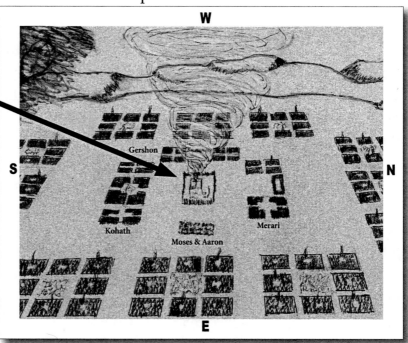

Illustration of Israel's encampment in the desert by artist D'Ann Medlin. Used by permission.

In the period of the New Covenant we are presently in, the Lord dwells within each believer, and as each believer moves out into the "world" or the "marketplace" to enthrone His sovereignty there, the enemy's strategy is the same as it was then: *to defile the place reserved for the King.*

Aleeyah, I believe that the Lord has called you as a levitical leader among your people. I encourage you, therefore, to read *The Levitical Calling*, for it is a foundational book. I pray that some of the principles I share here regarding the levitical calling are of help to you. We must not be ignorant of the wiles of the enemy. As I have studied the nature of *creatives* [those gifted and called to the arts] and *Levites* over the years, I want to bring to your attention seven key principles.

Principle #1: Some believers are more "wired" to spirit than others.

We were *wired* by our Creator to be able to hear Him and receive revelation from Him. When Adam and Eve fell, that ability to "hear God" was cut off. Mankind was prevented from hearing the full range of God's voice, even though we were given the ability to do so. In my study of the creative temperament, I call such people "creatives." Creatives are genetically given a greater ability to hear divine revelation.

This is why those in the arts and entertainment sectors have a much more difficult time fitting in with "normal" folks. We <u>are</u> different. We <u>hear</u> differently from other people. God made us this way. *Creatives* are musicians, dancers, performers, entrepreneurs, inventors and visionaries. We have an inner beacon that is very responsive to spiritual data…both good and evil.

This is why gifted artists are easily tormented. We are sensitive light-carriers whom God places in an dark, evil world. He intends, of course, that we look to Him to develop this discerning gift and expand His Light <u>into</u> the darkness...spreading the Kingdom of God. As you can imagine, the enemy does not want this. Therefore, knowing how sensitive creatives are to spirit, he has developed brilliant strategies in an attempt to destroy us and throw us off course. We are targeted for destruction <u>because</u> we have within our very make-up the ability to *hear* inspired revelation from the Father. The enemy cannot create...he copies, mimics and steals. Thus, he despises the creative temperament and delights when we fall.

Principle #2: Levites are wired this way as well…especially Kohathites.

Kohathites are those Levites who were positioned South of the Tabernacle. They were assigned to carry on their bodies the holy things of God: the Ark of the Covenant, the menorah, the lavers, the altars, the showbread. The Kohathites were assigned to function inside the Tabernacle, closest to the presence of God. Their job was to assist the priests. In our present day understanding of the levitical call, Kohathites are your worshippers, dancers, musicians, composers, intercessors, teachers of the Word of God, and deliverance ministers.

One principle we see is that a Kohathite literally "carries" in his body the burden of his assignment. This relates to today's role of bearing burdens of intercession on behalf of the people. Kohathites play a critical role in ministering to the Lord by serving His people and bringing them and their burdens into His presence. It stands to reason, therefore, that the enemy would especially attempt to defile this group of people.

Here's his strategy: The enemy seeks to locate any open doors to defile a Levite. Defilement usually comes about in one of three ways:

1. Through the person's choice to sin and go the way of the flesh.

2. Through generational iniquity, whereby an ancestor [known or unknown] has walked contrary to the Lord and done certain things. This creates a weakness or inherited tendency for the person in a subsequent generation to do the same thing. This is what is meant by God's *"visiting the iniquity of the fathers upon the children to the third and fourth generation of those who hate me, but showing steadfast love to thousands of those who love me and keep my commandments."* (Exodus 20:5-6)

3. Through contact with someone who carries or exudes a defiling spirit.

The Lord is always at work in our lives, pointing out areas of darkness where the enemy has constructed strongholds, or weak areas wherein we are prone to fall. This "pointing out" weak areas is one of the jobs of Holy Spirit. When we see where the enemy has gained ground, our responsibility as Levites is to forsake and renounce that thing. Or, we are to seek levitical examination and cleansing from someone more mature, who is gifted in discernment. This "cleansing process" lasts a lifetime. The more of God's glory He allows us to carry, the more we need to be "cleansed" and "purged," because our spiritual eyes will become more sensitive to defilement.

Principle #3: Creatives and Levites have very sensitive spirits.

We are like spiritual barometers, if you will, called to live among an unclean people. We pick up the presence of spirits easily. Without a solid foundation in the Word of God, we can easily go off into New Age thinking, or wrong doctrines involving spirits. We need great wisdom how the nature of defilement operates.

Here's a typical scenario: a fledgling Levite goes into a work situation and picks up something in the atmosphere. Let's say it is a backbiting, critical spirit. All of a sudden, within this group she no longer feels safe. She looks at the other people and begins to imagine they are talking negatively about her. She leaves the event and returns home, only to think something must be wrong with her. She rehearses all her flaws and concludes that she really isn't the spiritual person she thought she was. She gets down on herself and her faith begins to weaken that God has really called her to anything. She has been defiled. The enemy has taken ground.

What has happened is that the sensitive "spiritual barometer" has gone into a situation and correctly picked up negative, backbiting spirits. What she doesn't yet understand is that she lacks the discerning ability to separate herself from "that spirit." That spirit becomes so real to her, in fact, that she begins to "own it," and now thinks that spirit is <u>her</u>!

Let me give you several examples of how this insidious tactic operates:

<u>#1</u> One Thanksgiving I invited several friends who had nowhere else to go. I was in good spirits at the beginning of the event. During dinner, one of those friends – a success coach – talked incessantly about her clients and how they were now earning six figures. She went on and on about how she was being used to bring them incredible success. As I was washing dishes when everyone went home, my mood had changed totally. I looked at my life and saw squat. I felt like a failure, that whatever I thought I was accomplishing for

the Lord paled in comparison to her success. In spiritual terms, I not only had "picked up a spirit of inferiority" which was manifesting in her, but I began to "own it" and conclude it was me. That is defilement.

#2 John Sandford, co-founder of Elijah House Ministries – a pioneering work in the inner healing and deliverance movement – once told a story about recognizing a defiling spirit and dealing with it on the spot. Typically, he and his wife Paula counseled people together...but one day, Paula was not able to join him. In the middle of counseling a young woman, suddenly John began to have sexual thoughts toward her. *What was going on here?* He was in the midst of being defiled by a "spirit of fornication." As a sensitive Levite, he was accurately picking up the evil spirit. Wise and discerning man that he is, however, he faced the spirit head on. He asked the young woman point blank, *"Are you having sexual thoughts toward me?"* She hung her head and admitted that she was. He immediately took authority over that spirit and cast it away from her and out of the counseling room. The unclean spirit was gone and he continued with the ministry work to which he had been called. Tell me, how many untold pastors and counselors have experienced similar circumstances and gone on to have affairs, left their spouses and split their churches? They were defiled! The enemy found an open door and the Levites were ignorant in how to do battle.

#3 I went on a business trip with a colleague – one who did not walk with the Lord. The entire time we were driving, this colleague was pressuring me to give him a monetary advance on an upcoming job. The pressure was relentless. By the time I got home, I was an emotional wreck. I was no longer walking in the peace of God that was in my heart when the trip began. When I began paying bills, I became overwhelmed with angst over whatever financial situation lay before me. I was so worked up that I found it hard to pray. I tried talking with my pastor, but continued to feel overwrought. I finally said, *"I need to hang up. I need to go before the Lord and find out what this is."* I got before the Lord and poured out this avalanche of emotion, anxiety and worry. I have learned to pay attention to times like this when the peace of God is no longer in control. I waited in silence before the Lord. Finally, the truth began to dawn in my soul: I had been defiled by the "spirit of financial anxiety" that was consuming this man. As a Levite, I had discerned the spirit correctly....but as one who is still learning to walk the levitical walk, I did not separate myself from that spirit. Rather, I began to "own the spirit" for myself. That is defilement.

Do you see the enemy tactic? If he can get our eyes off Jesus, and the authority we have as we walk with Him, we become like everyone else, and we fall prey to an unclean spirit ourselves. What I should have done was to recognize the spirit yet remain detached from it…then ask the man if I could pray for him and cast away that spirit of anxiety that was plaguing him. This is what is meant by walking the levitical walk in a world where evil spirits are not just adding to each other… they are <u>multiplying</u>!

Principle #5: The way to walk before the Lord and keep ourselves unstained is to recognize our own "body tells" and cast unclean spirits away.

We must learn to walk in the authority of Jesus. He has given us power to cast out spirits. The next step is to recognize our "body tells" when we are in the presence of a defiling spirit. Some people smell sulfur when around demons. Others feel an oppressive heaviness. My pastor can sense immediately when we've crossed the border into another county, one that is filled with unclean spirits. For me, my "body tell" is that my inner spirit gets in turmoil. Whatever it is, the Lord will teach you to discern good from evil as it says in Hebrews 5:14. We must be trained – as we are in the levitical bootcamp – how to walk in the world and keep ourselves unstained by it, and to free others who are being likewise attacked.

Principle #6: The more we carry God's anointing, the bigger the demonic attack we will experience.

We will never get to the place where we have "arrived" spiritually. When Jesus walked the earth, He was God in the flesh. Everywhere He went, demons manifested. We must learn to expect to see manifestations of demons…and to walk confidently that Holy Spirit will help us discern quickly what spirit is in operation and cast it away.

Aleeyah, think about it this way as you give direction to your children: God has designed the polarity of holy and evil spirits because Light always reveals and exposes Darkness. The more Light you carry…the more Darkness will be revealed. God allows this because His desire for us as Levites is to cast away the darkness as we move into the part of secular culture to which we have been assigned. In a secular setting, we may be limited in how we go about casting out evil spirits…but it can still be done. I was recently in a business situation wherein I saw a spirit manifesting. I got off by myself and began to war against that spirit. I took authority over it and shut it up in the name and authority of Jesus. Then I went on about my business, refusing to let my mind dwell in that "negativity."

Principle #7: We need to be cautious about the people we let into our lives.

This is a time of separation between the Levites and the Church…a time when those called as Levites are being identified and trained in the divine bootcamp. Not every Hebrew that came out of Egypt was a Levite. In the same manner, not every Christian has a levitical calling. Caution your children to be on the alert if the Lord begins to separate them from some they used to call "friends." For example, this is an especially trying time for women whose spouses are under the control of defiling spirits. This is a dangerous situation… especially if the woman knows with all her heart that God is calling her into a deeper place with Him. I am not advocating divorce when she has no grounds to do so. We are to live our lives as becoming the Lord, even among those who may not be walking with Him. This walk is not easy. If a woman finds herself in this situation, it is critical to surround herself with godly mentors who will intercede for her and be observant if she begins manifesting negative spirits.

Just recently I was at a party. While talking with a fellow *creative*, I noticed that her usual joy and enthusiasm about her work were gone. I asked, *"When did you begin to think you weren't gifted as an artist?"* She seemed shocked that I saw her struggling with her self-esteem. When I got home, the Lord began to teach me more about walking as a Levite. He asked me to pray for her, to come against those spirits that were trying to tear her down. He gave me yet another lesson in how we minister to the Lord by ministering to His children.

This work is done most often in the closet, away from the public eye. Levites are, above all, *servants* of Jesus Christ. We are called to serve Him, and we serve Him most by lifting up His children who *"struggle not against flesh and blood, but against the spiritual forces of wickedness in high places."* (Ephesians 6:12)

Jesus said in John 4:24, *"God is Spirit and those who worship Him must worship Him in spirit and in truth."* As we walk in His Spirit, we worship Him by taking authority over every spirit that raises up against the knowledge of God. I want to encourage you, Aleeyah, that as you learn how to live as a Levite, embrace this incredible calling. The Lord has entrusted you with <u>every</u> authority to cast out spirits that are harassing your children.

SUGGESTED PRAYER

"Holy Father, please light the candle of understanding within me and give me discernment when I am being defiled by unclean spirits. Help me to spiritually read my own "body tells." You promised in your Word to protect me from the snare of the fowler, and that no evil will befall me because I know Your Name. I place myself in the shadow of the Almighty and in the shelter of the Most High. Thank You for your divine protection. (Psalms 91) I trust that you will present me and my children without blemish before the presence of Your glory in the final day. In the name of Jesus Christ, my Deliverer. Amen. (Jude 24-25)

LETTER 10
The Sexual Assault On The Church

Dear Aleeyah,

This subject matter has gripped me with an acute sense of alarm. In fact, this chapter is taken from a two-part article I wrote in 2011, which ended up going viral. It was inspired by a report from *Charisma* Magazine estimating that up to 40 percent of American pastors view pornography every day. Louisiana pastor Larry Stockstill shared with attendees of Charisma Media's Orlando Summit on Integrity, *"The Lord told me we're going to lose our nation if we don't turn our pastors around."* The sheer numbers of Christian leaders who are falling due to moral failure is staggering.

Even though some of the illustrations I use here refer to specific black churches, please understand that this sexual attack is targeting ALL churches, regardless of race. I have chosen these examples because I believe that my brothers and sisters of color are under an unprecedented attack, and the Lord has given me some insight as to why...and why <u>now</u>.

I am sure you read about the lawsuits of four young men against Bishop Eddie Long, pastor of New Birth Missionary Baptist Church in Atlanta, for allegedly using his position to engage in homosexual acts with them. Because I live in Atlanta, I am familiar with this situation. In fact, several friends attended this church...and I was concerned about what may be happening to those sitting in the pew while Bishop Long continued to function as pastor and preacher. I prayed for my friends and for the situation, and spoke with others seeking answers and insight.

Shortly after the scandal broke, my new subscription arrived of a magazine, which targets African American churchgoers. Bishop Long's picture was on the cover with the headline, *"When Scandal Rocks Your Church."* I thought to myself, *"Finally, someone is going to address this matter and give a solid biblical perspective."* Sadly, there was very little commentary or biblical analysis...little more than I would read in the *National Enquirer*.

The next month's issue came and featured two salient headlines: *"Sex & Sexuality, The Revolution"* and *"Life After The Down Low, One Woman's Story."* Once again, I read the magazine from cover to cover, anxious to find <u>somebody</u> giving biblical insight into what I perceive to be a machine gun blast of perversion aimed at the black church. So as not to be overly critical, their failure to address this issue is most likely due to ignorance of the acutely sensitive nature of those whom God has chosen to minister in churches through the arts.

My Vantage Point Is Unique

Having been in the Arts for so long, I have become an active spokesperson for two people groups relative to this issue:

1. *Those gifted and anointed in the arts.* Our churches are filled with "creatives" as worship leaders, dancers, musicians and singers. We are assigned to the altar, and charged with leading others into the presence of the Lord.

2. *Those called as modern-day Levites.* Levites are those who know in the depth of our being that we are called to serve the Lord Jesus when He returns. Our levitical forefathers endured the "divine bootcamp" of the wilderness for our benefit. They learned how to become a ministerial buffer between a defiled people and a holy God. Like them, many of us have found ourselves in the unfamiliar territory of a wilderness not of our own choosing. We have had to undergo intense refining and testing...and have come alive once we were reconnected to our Jewish roots and embraced our calling as Levites.

Aleeyah, allow me to share eight biblical principles that are specifically related to this assault of sexual perversion...principles that are not understood by the majority of church leaders. Sadly, the failure to take heed to them lies at the very root of this immorality epidemic.

Principle #1: The Enemy's Strategy To Defile Levites

The previous chapter explained what defilement is, but I want you to see just how defilement operates at all-too-many altars of the church and brings about the enemy's true goal.

Here's a common scenario:

Let's imagine a worship leader is hanging out with a male friend who, unbeknownst to him, carries a homosexual spirit. As a *creative*, the worship leader's spiritually sensitive nature picks up something and all of a sudden he feels things he never felt before. Remember, he is *wired* by God to pick up spiritual data...that is his GIFT...but no one talks from the pulpit about how to operate effectively in it, and warned what to watch out for. He is totally unprepared for what is about to happen.

Out of "nowhere," he becomes sexually aroused just talking with the guy and wonders in his private thoughts what certain experiences would feel like. Because he hasn't been spending a lot of time with the Lord lately, his faith is not built up. Maybe he's even feeling like a failure with women, since he can't seem to connect with his girlfriend. So...rather than look at his friend, discern the "spirit" operating in him and say (even silently), *"I recognize you...you're a homosexual spirit. I cast you away from me in the name and the authority of Jesus Christ,"* he continues to be obsessed with questions: *Why am I feeling this way? Oh God, there must be homosexual tendencies in me! Maybe that's why I'm not happy with my girlfriend.*

This worship leader does not understand that part of the call of being a *creative* and a Levite is to be fully aware of the unclean spirits around him, discern what spirits they are and cast them away. That's why he was given such a spiritually sensitive spirit in the first place...to <u>"clean house!"</u> However, this worship leader is young...and everyone looks up to him because of his giftedness. He is a prime target for being defiled. Besides, who in the world is he going to confess his thought life to...his pastor!?

Sadly, the more he obsesses with his own self-doubts, the more that spirit has lured him into its web. He dreams about these new feelings all night, tossing and turning... wondering if it's true: *Am I gay?*

Should he act on the impulse in a weak moment, a door to the homosexual stronghold is flung wide open. To return to "normal" becomes a much more difficult journey... because now the cellular memory of the pathway to sexual pleasure has been corrupted. That's why the Apostle Paul says, *"Every other sin that a man commits is outside his body, but he who commits adultery* (i.e., fornication) *sins against his own body."* (I Corinthians 6:18)

Once a specific cellular memory pattern is imprinted, the body automatically elicits a physical response whenever it is triggered by a similar feeling. In other words, once he experiences sexual pleasure in a homosexual encounter (even molestation as a young boy, or spankings where the nerves in the buttocks stimulate the genital area), his thoughts and body will want to go <u>there</u> again. Years can go by and even though he may marry and desire to enjoy lovemaking with his wife...his body remembers something else...he longs for it. He has been defiled.

Principle #2: Music Carries Spirit

When someone prays, preaches, prophesies, declares, sings by the power of the Holy Spirit, the recipient responds to the anointing the person carries. That's because we were made to receive direct words from the Father into our spirits. The converse is also true. If a singer, for example, sings a worship song, and she was fornicating with her lover the night before, she will broadcast a spirit of fornication from the altar into the congregation.

What happens then is that the entire congregation is defiled because they are sitting of their own free will and opening themselves up to whatever is coming from the altar. They're hardly expecting a spirit of lust! They're looking for intimacy with God.

A friend of mine who was part of the intercessory team of one of Atlanta's megachurches told me that one day after church, a security car was patrolling the parking lot and found a couple fornicating in a car, in broad daylight! The pastor heard about it and blasted the congregation the following week. But what had really happened? Someone had likely been defiled by a spirit of fornication by someone who was broadcasting it through song, or dance, or a musical instrument. In other words, the evil spirit attached itself to the medium of expression (the song) and went straight into the spirits of the unsuspecting members in the congregation...and landed into one who had a lustful predisposition through an unruly thought life. Such is the way of defilement.

Principle #3: The Levitical Mandate To Guard The Purity Of The Altar

Earlier, you saw how the Levites were encamped around the Tabernacle. God requires a people who are clean and undefiled in order to dwell in our midst. He thus trains His Levites to become a buffer between a Holy God and a sinful people.

What would the enemy do to keep God away from a worship service?

Defile the Levites.

This is exactly what is happening in the Church. The enemy's prime target is whoever is participating at the altar (pastor, worship leader, singers, musicians, dancers).

Artist: D'Ann Medlin. Used by permission.

The Word teaches that when there is defilement, the Holy Spirit leaves, and a door opens for the unclean spirits to defile those who are sitting in the pew.

Artist: D'Ann Medlin. Used by permission.

Any spirit seeks a medium of expression to work through. If a church sows seeds of immorality and broadcasts spirits of fornication from the altar, the church will reap fornication in the people.

The spiritual discipline of cleansing was required of Priests and Levites whose turn it was to minister before the Lord. One week prior to their time of service they came to the Temple and purified themselves. They well understood that if they were unclean, they risked death from a holy God who demands purity and lack of defilement from His servants. This is a depiction of the inner chamber of the Temple where levitical priests were ritually cleansed.

Principle #4: When A Church's Altar Is Defiled

Recently, I heard the powerful testimony of a truly gifted worship leader: composer, arranger, producer, singer and musician: Terry MacAlmon. Terry is multi-gifted, and for years served as worship leader for international ministries such as Benny Hinn's. Anyone who has been in a worship experience with him knows that Terry is anointed to bring people into God's presence.

So, leaders did what "the world" does all the time: they tried to "buy that anointing" by hiring Terry as worship leader. You can imagine how leaders clamored around him. If they could get Terry MacAlmon for their event, it would be a sell-out...people would be moved in the worship experience...and, give more money to the ministry.

Other musicians pressed in to befriend him and puff him up with flattery, hoping some drip of his anointing would fall on them. Such is the life of one who walks in great giftedness.

One day, word got out that Terry had "stepped down" in the midst of a sexual scandal. Rumors buzzed. The Body of Christ had lost another Levite who had problems walking in his giftedness.

At long last, Terry re-surfaced from disgrace and was asked to speak to a sparsely-attended group of men at a predominantly women's conference that my pastor attended. She wasn't allowed to attend his "men-only" talk...but she bought the DVD of the meeting. There she and I sat, when she returned home from the conference, glued to the television screen listening to his every word.

I did not write down word for word what Terry said, but this is the gist of his message to those men: *"I was given a powerful anointing to bring people into the presence of God... but everyone put me on a pedestal. I was showered with adoration, praise and money...I was sought after by leaders wanting me to align with their ministries. It was very seductive...and slowly, I began to lose something I never dreamed I would lose: <u>I lost my reverence for God.</u> I began to take my giftedness for granted, and felt entitled to the attention, the praise and material trappings. My pride caused me to fall in the worst possible way and hurt many people. I lost my marriage, my family, my reputation, and everything else dear to me."*

The biblical reason Terry lost the fear of God is that **the Spirit of the Fear of the Lord had left the building!**

Many may not recall that Terry's acclaim as a worship leader grew when he served under Ted Haggard, the Colorado Springs pastor who fell from grace through homosexual encounters he had engaged in for years. The spirit of homosexuality had defiled Haggard, and that fornicating spirit in Haggard defiled the altar of the church...the altar where Terry ministered.

The Word of God teaches that there are seven (7) spirits that *flow* from the throne of God, one of which is the spirit of the Fear of the Lord.* The departure of this spirit brought about Terry's implosion. In Rev. 5:6, John writes, *"I beheld and lo, in the midst of the elders, stood a Lamb as it had been slain, having seven horns and seven eyes, which are the seven Spirits of God sent forth into all the earth."* In these latter days, Jesus Himself as the Lamb of God, is sending forth these seven Spirits which are listed in Isaiah 11:2.*

The principle is that when there is defilement in an assembly of God's people, the presence of the Lord <u>leaves</u>! This begs the question: If the Spirit of the Lord leaves a defiled church, shouldn't <u>we</u>?!

I believe Scripture teaches that when there is corroborated evidence of immorality in the leadership of a church:

Leave The Church Immediately!

"Let not immorality or any uncleanness...<u>be heard of</u> among you...do not be partakers with them." (Ephesians 5:3, 7) Also in I Corinthians 5:1, *"It is <u>reported</u> that immorality is common among you..."* (emphasis mine) Both of these cases were corroborated "heresay." In the latter example, the Apostle Paul went so far as to say, *"I have already judged him...and delivered him over to Satan for the destruction of his body."* (I Corinthians 5:3-5)

To remain at such a church is to risk exposure to you and your family from defiling spirits and powerful principalities that now have access to the altar. If you do not leave, I believe that very soon, it may be impossible to do so.

* These 7 spirits are mentioned in Isaiah 11:2 – Spirit of the Lord [mercy], Wisdom, Understanding, Counsel, Might, Knowledge and the Fear of the Lord.

In like manner, if there is evidence that immorality exists among any of the creatives ministering at the altar (worship leaders, singers, dancers, musicians):

> *See to it they are made to step down and not serve until they have shown true repentance, and a lifestyle of purity is restored!*

It is critical in these evil days not to compromise one ounce of His glory that we have been entrusted with.

Principle #5: How False Doctrine Forms

When someone sins, and enjoys that sin, he or she deals with it in one of three ways:

1. Repents and renounces all participation with that sin.
2. Stays in it and risks discipline and judgment from a holy God.
3. Builds a false doctrine around the sin to make doing it easier to live with.

This third option is where many churches find themselves regarding the sin of homosexuality. As you well know, Aleeyah, both the Old and New Testaments call homosexuality <u>sin</u>. (Leviticus 20:13; Romans 1:26-27)

What has happened in our licentious culture is that doctrine is changing to accommodate those who have the desire to live a homosexual lifestyle. For example, many now believe that God actually creates some people to be gay...that it is an acceptable alternate lifestyle...that it is a "state of being" dictated by God-given genetics.

<u>This is a false doctrine</u>.

God would never lead or create a person to become what He has strictly forbidden in His Word. Scripture teaches plainly that *"The unrighteous will not inherit the Kingdom of God. Do not be deceived; neither the <u>fornicators</u>* [*pornos* = "male prostitutes"], *nor idolators, nor <u>adulterers</u>* [*moichos* = "male paramours"], *nor <u>homosexuals</u>* [men who lie with males], *...will <u>inherit</u>* [*kleronomeo* = "obtain by inheritance a portion secured from the patrimony"] *the Kingdom of God."* It doesn't get much clearer than this. God did not make a mistake when He created us as male and female.

The question arises, *What about all the people who report that from a young age, they felt like they were in the wrong body? Are they crazy?* No. *Has God changed His mind?* No. *Is there a divine clause floating around in the ether that provides an "escape clause" to gays, lesbians, transvestites and transgendered men and women?* No. The truth is: there **are** biblical explanations as to why so many feel they are "in the wrong body." Make no mistake about it - this is a genuine experience, and produces inordinate sexual conflict within a person. Hopefully the next two principles will shed further light on this issue.

Principle #6: Generational Sin

The second commandment states plainly that to those who bow down and serve anyone or anything other than the Lord God, He will *"visit the iniquity of the fathers upon the children to the third and the fourth generation of those who hate me..."* (Exodus 20:5-6) When someone struggles with sexually aberrant desires and leanings, the high probability is that ancestral iniquity has been left unrepentant, and that iniquity is still in the blood. It is alive! If Able's blood [defiled by the spirit of murder] cried out to God from the ground [Genesis 4:10], so too can the sin of ancestral sexual perversion cry out in our bodies. The Lord says that the *"life is in the blood."* (Leviticus 17:14)

Sexual perversion is seductive. From the very beginning, the Israelites struggled with the sexual addiction that ran rampant in Baal worship. Male and female prostitution were commonplace, and the false theology of this god not only allowed for the combination of worship and sexual pleasure, but underlined it. This sort of perversion lives on in the bloodline if our ancestors practiced it. It lies dormant in the DNA, waiting for the right circumstances to come along to allow it to manifest.

Ancestral iniquity explains why some people have stronger proclivities toward alcoholism, poverty, addictions, illegitimacy, divorce, violence, adultery, incest, bestiality and yes, homosexuality. As our generations get further and further away from following God's ways, we will see an even greater manifestation of perversion.

Jesus said, *"As were the days of Noah, so will be the coming of the Son of man."* (Matthew 24:37) [Emphasis mine] What were the days of Noah like? The earth was so perverse with fornications, adultery, homosexuality, incest, pedophilia, orgies, sodomy and bestiality that God called for a Flood to cleanse the earth from the filth. Jesus said that as it was then, so it will be again before He returns.

The good news is that there <u>is</u> a biblical way to cleanse ourselves from ancestral sins. It is a spiritual discipline called <u>*identificational repentance*</u> and is illustrated beautifully in Leviticus 26:40, Nehemiah 9 and Daniel 9. Galatians 3:13 says that *"Christ redeemed us from the curse of the law, having become a curse for us."* Notwithstanding this glorious truth, it is still each person's individual responsibility before God to repent for our own ancestral iniquity and bring our forefathers' specific sins before Him to be cleansed.

I devote an entire chapter to *"Generational Cleansing"* because I believe it is one of the most ignored and important of all the spiritual disciplines. My life was literally transformed when I repented for my own ancestral sins...and I had walked with the Lord over 30 years before I came to understand this truth!

Principle #7: The Power Of An Inner Vow

This principle is illustrated beautifully by the story of a sensitive man called to be a Levite.

The Mark Sandford Story

Mark Sandford, son of noted inner healing and deliverance pioneers, John and Paula Sandford (Founders of Elijah House Ministries), was gang raped at the age of 5 by a group of teenage boys. He bore the horrible secret deep within his psyche. He pushed the memory so far down that he had no recollection of it. In other words, his conscious mind dissociated from the memory altogether. As he grew older, he walked into the kitchen one day and announced to his mother, *"I've decided I don't want to be a boy...I'm going to be a girl."* Paula was stunned. The only thing she could say was, *"Well, too bad...God made you a little boy, and that's what you are!"*

As the months went by, Mark began to be transformed into a little girl. He let his hair grow, and he took on feminine characteristics. He talked like a girl...walked like one... looked like one. Kids at school called him a "fag" and made his life miserable. We see this phenomenon more and more in today's culture. As you can imagine, John and Paula were beside themselves, because nearly every week someone at church would say, *"You have the most adorable little girl!"*

The full story is a miraculous one...but allow me to summarize by saying that years later, through the ministry of Holy Spirit revealing a Word of Knowledge to an anointed counselor, the memory began to surface. Mark then began his long journey toward inner healing and the breaking of inner vows. Now happily married, with children, Mark heads up Elijah House Ministries. He knows firsthand the power of an inner vow. He recalls now that after the rape, he made one: *"If this is what it is to be a boy, then I refuse to be one. I will be a girl."*

That inner vow was so strong that it was able to alter the very cells and hormones of his being. Remember the biblical admonition of the power of the tongue and verbal confessions we allow to proceed out of the mouth. (James 3)

The good news is that there is total healing and deliverance when someone is involved in or perpetrated by the spirit of homosexuality, for it is the Father's heart to set His children free. The voices of those who have been so delivered have never been more needed now!

Principle #8: How Doors Are Opened To Principalities of Perversion

The enemy cannot gain a foothold in someone's life, or in one's ancestral line unless a door has been opened by willful disobedience and rebellion. Spiritual forces of wickedness are divided into ranks or degrees of power: evil spirits, fallen angels, spiritual hosts of wickedness, powers, world rulers of darkness and principalities. There is a tightly layered hierarchy of evil. (Ephesians 6)

The more a family line, a city or a region opens the door to a particular sin, the sheer numbers of these powers of darkness over those spirits increase – so much so that entire regions become "branded" by specific principalities.

For example, New York is known for its love affair with greed, the spirit of mammon. Hollywood has more strongholds than stars: immorality, gossip, adultery, homosexuality, anorexia, and countless others. The manifestation of these spirits grows proportionately to the sheer numbers of people who willfully give themselves over to manifest those spirits. Until now, San Francisco was known as the "capital of homosexuality." It has recently been reported that Atlanta now has more homosexuals than any other city in the U.S.

There are reasons why.

#1- *Through Government Leaders:*

During the time leading up to the grand opening of the Georgia Aquarium, Atlanta was going through a "re-branding." City leaders spent millions of dollars to make sure they positioned Atlanta correctly and communicated its message to the desired demographic. Being the owner of a 28-year old ad agency and consultant to countless businesses over the years, I am especially interested in the principles involved in effective marketing and branding of an entity...so I followed this "re-branding of Atlanta" with much interest.

Both the *Atlanta Journal & Constitution* and the *Atlanta Business Chronicle* reported this story diligently. One day, the city's leaders proudly announced their desired demographics: <u>blacks and homosexuals</u>! What these leaders failed to realize is that government authorities have the power to open doors to demonic principalities. They announced through every available media, *"We want blacks...and we want homosexuals here!"* There should be no surprise, therefore, to witness the fallout of a spirit of homosexuality allegedly defiling one of Atlanta's most beloved black pastors.

2- *Through Moral Compromise:*

It is common knowledge that many churches hire the best musicians because they believe that's why many come to church in the first place: to hear good music. Pastors reason, *"If we don't have great music, the people will go somewhere else."* The unspoken reality is, *"They'll go **tithe** someplace else."* So, to ensure that the coffers will be full, churches often hire the best in town regardless of whether those musicians are walking with the Lord or not.

The musicians then show up at church as another paying gig. They reason, *"I believe in Jesus..I need to be in church anyway...so why not get paid for it?"* The likelihood, though, is that musician played at a club the night before, picked up all sorts of defiling spirits (fornication, lust, homosexuality, alcoholism, anger, jealousy, lawlessness, rebellion), brought them into the altar, and broadcast them to the people. Is it any wonder our churches are a breeding ground for divorce, gangs, addictions and unbridled lust?

What happens if a young dancer gets pregnant outside of marriage? Does the worship leader make her quit dancing until she has fully repented for her immorality? I'd bet not. What if the worship leader is carrying on with the lead singer? Anybody dare to fire him? I don't think so...especially if he is a recording icon whom the people come every week to hear.

So...What do you do with a pastor who faces allegations involving perversion? If the pastor's job before God is to guard the purity of the altar...and if he is potentially guilty of defiling that altar, what are the people to do if there is no governing board to hold the pastor accountable?

A PROPHETIC DREAM: "Horror In The Church"
(January 18, 2004)

As written in my dream journal.

I was in a small church. My husband was the pastor, it appeared, but he was sitting down and another man was preaching. His message was awful...it didn't ring true to me.

That preacher sat down. I then watched all kinds of horror take place: children ran up on the podium and played around with the organ. Parents were oblivious to their actions. For some reason, I got up to announce the preacher, supposedly preparing the way not for the liberal preacher in the pew but for my husband who was coming back in. I told everyone to turn to the book of Revelation. The liberal preacher was furious to see that he was being replaced by someone else.

I sat down and heard a voice announce, *"This is what this church deserves!"* Suddenly a tall, slender, "otherworldly" man-woman (transvestite-looking) person entered the sanctuary. "She" had on a whitish-blue robe. Her hair was short and silver, like Annie Lenox (a rock star of the 70's). She walked triumphantly down the aisle...I sensed evil. The crowd gasped. No one challenged her or got up to leave.

At the pulpit, she suddenly became naked and appeared to melt or puddle on the floor in a filmy sheen. I could see the outline of her body...her breasts were exposed. I tried to cover my child's eyes, but then decided to let him watch.

Much havoc followed. I kept waiting for someone to stand up and take charge, but no one did. I saw a big pile of excrement near where the woman's body was. People from the congregation took turns going down a slide right into it. There was filth and urine and all manner of foulness at the altar.

Suddenly I was outside the church. Someone faceless (typically an angel or Holy Spirit) was with me. It was dark and I was trying to get help. We walked past a house and a woman came out and walked beside me. She "appeared" to be one of the church leaders and knew I was going back to the church to help people get out. As we walked, I sensed she was not of the Lord. I turned to look at her and shouted, *"I praise the name of the Lord!"* As I shouted it over and over, she began to manifest demonically. Her features contorted and she became vile-looking. As I continued to yell my praise to the Lord, she could not stand to be near me, and ran off.

We got to the church and found it bolted shut. The people were trapped inside. The faceless man handed me some wire cutters and I was desperately trying to re-move the bolt. Suddenly, I heard something and turned around. The evil woman, some 20-feet away, threw a tear-gas type thing into the chimney of the church and fumes and smoke began spewing out. I knew if I didn't get the bolt unlatched, everyone inside would die.

I woke up.

Pertinent Observations on Dream Interpretation Symbolism

- Often, in a dream where there are many things happening, the Lord is showing chronological stages that have or will take place over time.

- My first husband was a pastor who fell away from his calling. He rep-resents an entire generation of pastors whom God called to shepherd His people...but were removed from service or sidelined because of immorality and/or error.

- The second pastor, the liberal, was the next generation of pastors who came forth. This stage was characterized by unruliness of children, no sound teaching, no anointing of the Holy Spirit, no fear of the Lord. This explains why so many people are leaving the traditional church.

The Interpretation As The Lord Gave Me

"You are watching the destruction of My Church, and have been witness to the stages it has undergone. The two men I had as your husbands (my second husband died suddenly in 1998) were called to lead My people. You witnessed them under attack, and their ministries destroyed. You have witnessed many in My church being lulled by ineffectual teaching, the lack of power of My Spirit and the failure to uplift My holy Name.

"The entrance of the woman is what this church deserves. It is a seducing spirit. The people have not followed My Word and their lives are characterized by licentiousness, rebellion, living for their own passions and pleasures, and unruliness in their families.

"Suddenly, with very little warning, I will send utter delusion into the Church. It will have the appearance of the supernatural, but its core will be vile and evil. You will recognize it and leave the church, but the majority will be mesmerized and deceived. The change in My people, or those who call themselves My people, will be dramatic. There will be all manner of vileness on my altar...immorality will run rampant...and for those who embrace it, there will be no escape. I will lock them in.

"There will be watchmen, like you, who witness this...but you will not be able to save them. You will be preserved safe, but you cannot rescue those destined for destruction. 'He who saved a people out of the land of Egypt, afterward destroyed those who did not believe.' (Jude 5)

"These are evil times and the transition into it will be quick. The people will be engulfed by a deception that forever seals their fate. This time is soon approaching. (Note: the dream was given 8 years ago.)

"When it does, you and people like you will be persecuted and hounded by those who appear to be like you...only you will see them manifest as you lift up My Name in praise. Keep praising and lifting up My Name. It is your only protection. 'The Lord knows how to rescue the godly from trial, and to keep the unrighteous under punishment until the day of judgment, and especially those who indulge in the lust of defiling passion and despise authority.' (2 Peter 2:9-10)

"You clearly saw the false, even though it appeared to be ethereal. It was a seductress, glorying in the flesh and nakedness at My altar, allowing filth, unruliness and rebellion against authority. Her head was not covered...she was not under submission to a holy God.

"You were alarmed. This dream is a call to prayer for My Church. You are in a brief period of revival where My Name is being proclaimed, and the airwaves are open to broadcasting. That time is short...make the most of it, for the days are evil."

Questions From Readers

Aleeyah, when this original article went viral, I received so much response from readers that I want to include their questions here:

Q: "What is the role of intercessors in a church where there are rumors of immorality and perversion? If they leave, aren't they forsaking their post and really leaving the altar unguarded?"

This is an excellent question, and a difficult one. I spoke with several friends in full time ministry to glean their wisdom. The role of an intercessor is part of their levitical call. It is in this place of intimate prayer when an intercessor pushes through into God's presence and experiences closeness with God that other believers rarely achieve. It is not that intercessors are better than other believers...it is simply a different calling.

I spoke with a pastor who was part of the intercessory team at a large megachurch many years ago. During their times of intercession, the Lord revealed to them there was defilement in the leadership. It was not specific...but both of their spirits were extremely troubled. Months went by and they were so troubled by the revelation of "sin in the camp," that they wrestled with whether or not they should leave. They went to a conference in another state...and one of the pastors gave this couple a spontaneous prophetic word. With no knowledge of them or their circumstances, the first words out of his mouth were, *"The Lord says it is not time to leave the church!"* They returned to their intercessory role for two more years. Rumors of the pastor's rampant adultery surfaced more and more. Their time in prayer grew more difficult. These two were prayer warriors, however. They knew how to press in and do battle with the enemy. The time came, however, when the

Lord clearly revealed to both of them that it was time to leave. His message to them was crystal clear: *"Leave!"*

Those called as intercessors must be sensitive to the Holy Spirit. He will use their presence to call for repentance and revival in the church, and in its leaders. The Lord is merciful, and slow to anger. His heart's desire is for restoration of the shepherd of the flock, and protection for the flock itself. But the time can come, as it did with this couple, when the Lord says, *"Enough...leave!"* In Acts 16:6-7, Luke recounts, *"They* [Paul and Timothy] *went through the region of Phrygia and Galatia, having been forbidden by the Holy Spirit to speak the word in Asia. And when they had come opposite Mysia, they attempted to go into Bithynia, but the Spirit of Jesus did not allow them."* The Holy Spirit **and** the Spirit of Jesus forbade them to speak to those cities. This was a form of divine discipline. The word of truth was kept from those Asian regions. If you have been called to intercede at a scandal-ridden church, seek the Lord with fasting and prayer. He will show you. To stay when He has clearly said *"Leave!"* is to risk your own spiritual health. As with Lot and his family, the signal will be very clear when divine judgment is about to fall on the church.

> *Q: "If we can agree that God will never leave us or forsake us, how can we say that anything we do will make God leave us?"*

To answer this question, let's consider two women: one does her best to walk with the Lord, but may not be very spiritually mature. To this one, the Lord is very much the Good Shepherd, gently convicting of sin as she learns the walk of faith. *"It is the Lord your God who goes with you; he will not fail you or forsake you."* (Deuteronomy 31:6) The other one keeps having sex outside of marriage, not really worrying about it because in her mind, she can just say a little prayer and go back to doing the same thing. God's always there... so no big deal. There is no inner responsiveness to Holy Spirit. This is a person who has no fear of God. God deals with this woman differently from the first.

In I Kings 9, Solomon had just finished building the house of the Lord and dedicated the Temple. The presence of God filled the place with unspeakable glory. But right after this, here is what the Lord told the King: *"I have hallowed for me this house which you have built to put my name there forever...but if you shall turn from following me, you or your children, and will not keep my commandments and my statutes which I have set before you, but go and*

serve other gods and worship them; then I will destroy Israel from the face of the land which I have given them; and this house which I have hallowed for my name will I cast out of my sight."
(I Kings 9:1-9) [Emphasis mine]

The Lord not only turned His back on the holy Temple, He called for enemies to destroy it...*twice!* The principle underlying this question is this: When we sincerely desire to walk with God, and are open to His instruction and discipline, He will most certainly never leave us. The walk of faith is a journey, a progression of maturity. As long as our hearts are turned toward Him, He will never leave! We endanger ourselves, however, if we begin to take lightly so great a salvation and lose our reverential fear of the Lord.

Q: "I struggled with your statement that a creative or a pastor can release defiling spirits on the congregation. If they have prayed for God's anointing, doesn't that mean they would release God's Spirit on the congregation and not the enemy's?"

Our levitical forefathers were required to go through countless rituals of cleansing, bathing, and changing of clothes when conducting worship and sacrifices for the people. Why? Because the Lord insisted on absolute cleansing from any outside defilement by those whose duty it was to preach, pray, read Scripture, sacrifice, play instruments, sing or dance. One of the levitical disciplines is to teach the difference between the clean and the unclean...the holy and the unholy. (Leviticus 10:10-11) To do any of those things in a defiled state resulted in death or disease. Leading His people in worship is very serious business to God. The Temple (i.e., church) was considered sacred. God has not changed. It is we who have lost the concept of *"working out our own salvation in fear and trembling."*
(Philippians 2:12)

Numbers 16 is a chilling account of what happened when a group of Kohathites (one of the levitical families) tried to minister in a state of rebellion against Moses' and Aaron's authority, believing that they, too, were quite capable of ministering to the people. *"Fire came forth from the Lord and consumed the two hundred and fifty men offering the incense."* (Numbers 16: 35)

Consider this issue from another angle, concerning Laws of Physics that the Lord established in the earth: as I wrote earlier, there is a strong relationship between sound waves and spirit. As an example, the Bible contains many warnings against false prophets and false teachers. Why? Weren't they just people saying a bunch of words? No. Those words carried a wrong spirit that endangered the people. There was explicit danger in exposing spiritual ears to a false or evil spirit that was operating within that person's heart and attaching itself to the physical "prophetic words" coming out of a Levite's mouth, or from his musical instrument.

A sound wave is an "expression" of one's heart, and Jesus said the heart is always in danger of being defiled. (Matthew 15) Sound is not a neutral thing, for it has the ability to speak to a person's spirit. That's why some music is anointed (i.e., carries the presence of Holy Spirit), and other music has the ability to incite riots or lascivious behavior. Music and preaching (sound waves) are not all created equal.

SUGGESTED PRAYER

"Father, we are living in such an evil day. You said this time would come, when evil is multiplying and the power of darkness is at hand. Please give me and my children keen discernment to recognize the unclean spirits invading our churches. Let us become Levites who guard the purity of the altar as You deserve. Give us boldness to stand up and speak out against whatever evil should proceed from these altars, and the courage to leave the church when You say, "Leave!" Keep us from spirits of delusion and spiritual slumber. Thank You for enlightening me about the levitical disciplines of our forefathers, and their willingness to be instructed by You, and pass down this knowledge to us. How I long for Your presence to dwell among us. Thank You for the blessed sacrifice of the Lord Jesus, my Savior. Amen.

LETTER 11
The Mysterious Parallel Between Blacks & Jews

Dear Aleeyah,

I have long been perplexed by similarities between the two people groups who appear to have suffered the most throughout history: the Jews and the Blacks. As this book was gestating inside of me, what I kept seeing was that both groups experienced almost the exact same things! I asked, *"Why, Lord?"* That question led me to dig deeper into the ancestral archives.

Interestingly, the answer to *"Why, Lord?"* actually goes back to what inspired this book to begin with: namely, the prophetic dream that showed me that the key to freedom for your children lies in your <u>alignment</u> with *Ariel*...Jerusalem...God's people. In other words, the Lord's heart is for the people of color to safely dwell <u>in</u> the "tents of Shem" and enjoy the fullness of the Abrahamic blessing. He desires unity between Blacks and Jews.

One Defining Moment For Both Races

For both the Jews and Blacks, there was indeed <u>one</u> defining moment throughout their histories. For the Jews, that moment was the Exodus...the miraculous deliverance of a people who suffered <u>400</u> years of enslavement, degradation, poverty, and powerlessness under the hands of a ruthless nation. Yes, there have been many other difficult periods in Jewish history, such as global anti-Semitism, the Babylonian captivity, the destruction of the Temple, twice...and lest we forget, the Holocaust. If students of history simply looked at what has happened over the centuries to this singular group of people, the last thing they would conclude is that they were God's "chosen," His beloved people! And yet, this is exactly what God appointed for them to suffer, to show His faithfulness to His covenantal promise amidst horrific enemy attacks...and His awesome power to deliver.

So, what was history's defining moment for people of color? Many would probably say it was when millions were snatched from their homes in Africa and forced to endure years of slavery, cruelty, disease, degradation, poverty and powerlessness at the hands of another race of people, in a land not their own. How many years? <u>Four hundred</u>!

Historical Parallels Between Jews and Blacks

I am not a statistician, but I do not believe it is a mere coincidence that these two people groups were called to endure such an identical, difficult journey.

See for yourself:

- *<u>Both endured 400 years of slavery:</u>* Prior to the Exodus, the Egyptians held the Jews captive for 400 years. (Genesis 15:13) Ironically, research shows that the Slave Trade era took place during the 16th – 19th centuries, concentrating the first 200 years in Europe, and the last 200 in the Americas. It may have started as early as 1450, and ended in 1850…a total of 400 years.

- *<u>Both were thrust out into a strange land.</u>* At the Exodus, 2 to 3 million Jews were thrust out of Egypt, heading **East**. According to the <u>Encyclopedia Britannica</u>, during the Slave Trade, over 10 million Blacks were cast out of Africa heading in all directions: 4 million via the Red Sea; 4 million via the Indian Ocean; 9 million via a Sahara Desert caravan; and 11 – 20 million via the Atlanta Ocean…heading **West**.

- *<u>Millions died in a holocaust</u>.* The word *holocaust* means "a great destruction resulting in the extensive loss of life." The Jews lost over 6 million during Hitler's holocaust. Likewise, millions of Blacks died in the Slave Trade, or *Maafa*, which means "holocaust" in Swahili.

- *<u>Both groups were betrayed by their Noahic brothers</u>.* Prior to the Exodus, the Hebrews [descendants of Shem] were betrayed by the Egyptians [descendants of Ham]. At the time of the Slave Trade, the Blacks [descendants of Ham] were betrayed primarily by Whites [descendants of Japheth].

- *<u>Both worshipped money, power and false gods</u>* prior to their holocausts.

- *Both were kept from their divine destiny.* The Jews' ultimate destiny was to offer praise and worship to the one true God, and teach the world His ways prior to the coming of Messiah. The pre-ordained destiny for those *"beyond the Rivers of Ethiopia"* is to bring a sacrifice of praise to the Lord in Jerusalem prior to Messiah's second coming. (Zephaniah 3:10)

- *Leaders had no regard for them as people.* Egyptians were cruel taskmasters to the Jews, and had no regard for their lives or their families. Likewise, a majority of white slave owners had little regard for Blacks, and took no thought of destroying their families.

- *Both received prophesies that they would be scattered throughout the world and be enslaved.* (Ezekiel 29 – 32 and Genesis 15)

- *Both wandered in a wilderness when finally released.* The Jews wandered 40 years in the wilderness before reaching the land of promise. Many Blacks are still in their wilderness wandering prior to reaching their land of promise.

- *Both are under enemy attack to defile their people and thereby render their praise ineffective.*

Observe this passage from Psalms 44. Strangely, it captures the heart of anguish over the psalmist's "apparent disregard" by the Father. Stranger yet, these verses could describe perfectly either group: Jews or Blacks.

> *"But now thou hast forsaken us and put us to shame, and goest not forth with our armies. But thou makest us to be defeated; and our enemies have plundered us. Thou hast sold us like sheep appointed for meat; and hast scattered us among the Gentiles. Thou has sold thy people as a bargain, and dost not profit by their exchange. Thou makest us a byword among the Gentiles, a shaking of the head among the nations. All the day long my disgrace is before me, and the shame of my face has covered me…All this is come upon us; yet have we not forgotten thee…"* [44]

For the Jewish people, these four hundred years of horror in Egypt were part of their calling – a divine assignment, if you will – in order to ultimately showcase the full glory of God's preservation and deliverance of His people at the Exodus.

As to the people of color: *Where is their reward?* I believe we are witnessing it now. It's not over yet. Many have arrived at a place of great favor, wealth and prominence. Others are still working their way through their wilderness. I believe this has been the impetus of my call to write this book, to encourage you in your journey.

I believe in the future promise of great blessings for your children, Aleeyah. God is the same yesterday, today and forever. And just as the Jews are still experiencing persecution and enemy threats, so are many Blacks. Yet, Scripture teaches us the final chapter… an awesome end time display of might from the Almighty Himself: the redemption of His remnant from the seed of Abraham, and the oneness that we will all find in Messiah.

What About Whites?

Because the Lord is just, He is mindful of the many sins we Whites have perpetuated against your people. The assignment of this book led my research into many painful episodes of my people inflicting horrible cruelty on yours. I have confessed those ancestral sins many times, and used biracial gatherings to speak humbly before my brothers and sisters of color asking forgiveness.

On the larger scale, I believe that we (as a nation) are in the process of receiving now and in the immediate future the punishment due us for our sins of racial prejudice and injustice against a people beloved of the Father. He will hold us accountable, and balance the scales of justice. I believe we are losing our dignity and power as a nation, racism being just one of many sins we have committed. Just as your children are still in the process of experiencing their full Exodus….so we Whites are still in the process of reaping the iniquity we have sown at your expense. There's no getting around it, Scripture is clear: God is no respecter of persons. He is not mocked. He plays no favorites regarding race. *"Whatever we sow, that we shall reap."* (Galatians 6:7)

But for all of us who belong to the Lord: our end is to be in unity.

The Biblical Principle Which Guarantees God's Blessing

Allow me to delve briefly into the core, overarching biblical principle that guarantees God's blessing. It was a covenantal promise the Lord made with Abraham, the father of all nations.

"I will bless those who bless you, and him who curses you I will curse; and by you <u>all the families of the earth shall bless themselves</u>."

(Genesis 12:3) [Emphasis mine]

The secret to receiving God's blessing is found in how a person or a nation deals with the Jews…God's people…the descendants of Abraham.

What follows are some examples of mistreatment of Jews by some of your ancestors and the resulting curses. In contrast, the chapter that follows highlights examples of when your people were greatly blessed because of the <u>favor</u> they showed to the Jews. God is faithful to His covenantal promise to Abraham.

Two Historical Time Periods That Triggered Curses

#1 EGYPT: The father of the people of color was Ham, one of the sons of Noah. Ham's second-born son, Mizraim, as seen in this diagram, was the father of Egypt. In fact, the name *Mizraim*, according to Merrill F. Unger, is the standing name for "Egypt," in which sense it occurs nearly eighty-seven times.[45] Even more specifically, the name refers to both Upper and Lower Egypt – a civilization that figures prominently throughout biblical history, and especially how it related to the Hebrew people. Egypt was once a powerful civilization. It was often a safe haven for our forefathers Abraham, Joseph, the

HAM			
I. Cush	**II. Mizraim**	**III. Phut**	**IV. Canaan**
1- Seba	1- Ludim		1- Sidon
2- Havilah	2- Anamim		2- Heth
3- Sabtah	3- Lehabim		3- Jebusite
4- Raamah	4- Naphtuhim		4- Amorite
Sheba & Dedan	5- Pathrusim		5- Girgasite
5- Sabtecha	6- Casluhim		6- Hivite
6- Nimrod	Philistim		7- Arkite
	7- Caphtorim		8- Sinite
			9- Arvadite
			10- Zemarite
			11- Hamathite

Source: *Unger's Bible Dictionary by Merrill F. Unger. Moody Press, 1969.*

twelve tribes that descended from Jacob, as well as our Lord during His infancy. God used the nation mightily and blessed it when they treated descendants of Abraham well.

Examples of mistreatment:

- Pharoah's enslavement of the Jews in Egypt. Exodus 1 records that Pharoah ordered the Hebrew male infants to be killed. The <u>Book of Jasher</u> records the lesser known story of how God cared for these little ones in miraculous ways: *"The Lord who had sworn to their ancestors to multiply them, sent one of his ministering angels which are in heaven to wash each child in water, to anoint and swathe it and to put into its hands two smooth stones from one of which it sucked milk and from the other honey, and he caused its hair to grow to its knees, by which it might cover itself; to comfort it and to cleave to it, through his compassion for it."*[44]

- This Egyptian cruelty – inspired by the demonic desire to kill off the Messianic line – worsened against the Hebrew children. *"The labor of Egypt strengthened upon the children of Israel in those days, and behold if one brick was deficient in any man's daily labor, the Egyptians took his youngest boy by force from his mother, and put him into the building in the place of the brick which his father had left wanting."*[45] In other words, the Egyptian civilization at that time was literally built upon the blood of thousands of Hebrew babies. The people turned a deaf ear to the infant cries coming from within the plaster of the palace walls. As I'm sure you see, these actions opened a huge door to curses that God foretold would come upon those who mistreated His own. Let's look at verse 14: *"But I will bring <u>judgment</u> on the nation which they serve..."* [Emphasis mine] Moreover, God promised Egypt would be *"the humblest of the kingdoms,"* (Ezekiel 29:15) and that He would *"scatter the Egyptians among the nations and disperse them through the countries."* (Ezekiel 30:23)

#2 NIMROD: The child born to Ham's eldest son, Cush, in his later years, was Nimrod. The <u>Book of Jasher</u> records, *"At that time the sons of men again began to rebel and transgress against God, and the child* (Nimrod) *grew up, and his father loved him exceedingly, for he was the son of his old age."* [46]

Aleeyah, to be very honest, there is much disagreement about the place of Nimrod in the ancestral records of your people. I will do my best to present the various viewpoints. I want you to be able to look at him from different views and decide for yourself.

1. The biblical record.

2. The historical books of antiquity (Book of Jasher and The Jewish Antiquities by Flavius Josephus).

3. Return To Glory (The Powerful Stirring of the Black Race) by Joel A. Freeman, Ph.D. and Don B. Griffin.

4. The Nephilim Agenda by Randy DeMain.

5. Battles of the Elohim (They Walked As Men) by Christian Harfouche, Ph.D. and Robin Harfouche, Ph.D.

The Biblical Record

Nimrod first appears in Genesis 10:8, *"Cush became the father of Nimrod; he was the first on earth to be a mighty man. He was a mighty hunter before the Lord; therefore it is said, 'Like Nimrod a mighty hunter before the Lord.'"* In I Chronicles 1:10, we read, *"Cush was the father of Nimrod; he began to be a mighty one in the earth."*

Nimrod is described four times as *mighty*. On the surface, that sounds good. We notice something interesting, though. Nimrod *began to be* <u>*mighty*</u>. In other translations, we read, *"Nimrod <u>became</u> a mighty hunter before the Lord,"* indicating that this quality of being *mighty* was a process. Let's look deeper. The Hebrew word for *mighty* in these verses is *gibbor* which means "warrior, tyrant, strong, giant."

Controversy Over Nimrod's Character

Many regard Nimrod as an imperialist tyrant. His name in Hebrew means "rebel," suggesting the concept of rebellion as descriptive of the character of this empire-builder (i.e., Babylon, Shinar, Nineveh – all were godless, immoral kingdoms built by Nimrod).

To Many Blacks, Nimrod Was A Hero

A popular book surfaced in the last decade: Return To Glory (The Powerful Stirring of the Black Race) by Joel A. Freeman, Ph.D. and Don B. Griffin. This book lists as endorsers some well-respected African-Americans: Bill Cosby, Julius Erving, boxing champion Joe Frazier and Dr. Tony Evans, Senior Pastor of Oak Cliff Bible Fellowship.

Here are a few quotes from this book to illustrate their view:

- *"The first great ruler of the world was a man named Nimrod...he was a gifted hunter, provided for the protection of the community. He was a liberator and a freedom fighter for all humanity. His physical talents were obviously great...Nimrod's courage was attributed to his relationship with God. We know this by the phrase 'before the Lord.'"* [47]

- *"Nimrod built his kingdom in the 'land of Shinar,' also known by historians as Sumer. The black Sumerians had 'superior intellectual qualities,' according to R.K. Harrison. Not only that, but they, too, have a legacy of founding civilizations. Along with Egypt and Ethiopia in Africa, the Sumerians were the first to achieve intellectual greatness. All of mankind is indebted to these great people for the knowledge they discovered and passed on to the rest of mankind.'"* [48]

- Nimrod founded the city of Babel. He said, *"Come, let us build for ourselves a city, and a tower whose top will reach into heaven, and let us make for ourselves a name; lest we be scattered abroad over the face of the whole earth."* (Genesis 11:4)

- *"The African-American male is a descendant of 'a long line of giants, unsurpassed by any people on earth!'"* [49]

To Other Scholars, Nimrod Was Evil

The Book of Jasher, the only one of the ancient historical books mentioned and recommended by the Bible, records Nimrod's treatment of Abraham.

- Nimrod grew so powerful that he ruled over all of the children of Noah. When he was forty, he made war with the children of Japheth. This was the year Abram was born. Abram's father, Terah, served Nimrod as the prince of his army. In fact, Terah held the highest position in Nimrod's kingdom. Jasher records, *"Nimrod did not go in the ways of the Lord, and he was more wicked than all the men that were before him, from the days of the flood until those days. The night Abraham was born, Nimrod's wise men saw a great star coming from the east, and the same star ran with great speed, and swallowed up four great stars, from the four sides of the heavens...and said to the king, 'This thing applies to the child that is born to Terah, who will grow up and multiply greatly, and become powerful, and kill all the kings of the earth, and inherit all their lands, he and his seed forever.'"* [50]

- The wise men advised King Nimrod to buy the child from Terah, and they would kill it. Terrified by the news, Terah *"hastened and took a child from one of his servants and brought that child to the king, pretending it was Abram. And the Lord was with Terah in this matter, that Nimrod might not cause Abram's death, and the king* [Nimrod] *took the child from Terah and with all his might dashed his head to the ground, for he thought it had been Abram; and this was concealed from him from that day, and it was forgotten by the king, as it was the will of Providence not to suffer Abram's death."* This was the reason Terah took the child Abram and hid him in a cave for ten years. [51]

- Jasher 12 records that Nimrod tried to kill Abram two other times, but God's miraculous hand rescued His servant, for it was through Abraham's seed that Messiah was to come.

- Randy DeMain in <u>The Nephilim Agenda</u>, wrote: *"Nimrod began to build cities as places for habitation for wicked and unclean spirits. Together they began to build a tower* [the Tower of Babel] *into the heavenlies providing safety above the flood line and access into heaven, thrones, and dominions for earthbound spirits. Nimrod was obsessed with establishing a kingdom that God could not destroy, and on destroying the Promised Seed."* [52]

- Josephus wrote, *"Nimrod persuaded mankind not to ascribe their happiness to God, but to think that his own excellency was the source of it."* [53]

- <u>The Targum of Jonathan</u>: *"From the foundation of the world none was ever found like Nimrod, powerful in hunting, and in rebellions against the Lord."*

- The Chaldee paraphrase of I Chronicles 1:10: *"Cush begat Nimrod, who began to prevail in wickedness, for he shed innocent blood, and rebelled against Jehovah."*

- Nimrod was the founder of Babylon, which partook of his character as being the great antagonist of God's trust and God's people. In Nimrod we see Satan's first attempt to raise up a human universal ruler of men. [54]

- Drs. Christian and Robin Harfouche in <u>Battles of the Elohim: They Walked As Men</u> trace the age-old battle between Jehovah and the god of this world, depicted most often as a two-horned bull, and goes by many names: Ba'al, Ashteroth, Astarte, Apis (a bull worshipped in Egypt), Bel-Merodach or Marduk (the god of Babylon), Adramelech (Assyria), Ashima, Molech and others.

Nimrod's kingdoms worshipped this two-horned god, whose "fruit of that spirit" were: idolatry, sexual perversion, licentiousness, lawlessness, enslavement of others, and rebellion against Jehovah.[55]

SUGGESTED PRAYER

"Holy Father, Your ways are just and You are righteous in judgment. How I grieve for what these forefathers did to Your people. I repent for the wickedness from the line of Mizraim. I repent for the evil done to your children. I confess all wickedness associated with Nimrod: his rebellion against You, his reliance upon his own strength rather than Yours, and his need for renown and glory. I confess every action he committed to destroy the messianic line.

In the authority of Jesus, I loose myself, my children and grandchildren from Ba'al, from Ashteroth, from Astarte, from Apis, from Bel-Merodach, from Marduk, from Adramelech, from Ashima, from Molech, and any other god who dares to replace my allegiance to You, the God of Abraham, Isaac and Jacob and Father of the Lord, Jesus Christ. You alone, Lord, do I serve. I place these sins under the blood of Jesus, and close all ancestral doors to defiling, demonic spirits, and to any and all fallen Watcher Angels in the name and authority of Jesus.

Thank You for the calling that is upon me and my people, and that Your eye is upon us. May we shine as Your light in the earth. In Jesus' name. Amen.

LETTER 12
When Blacks Were Blessed

Dear Aleeyah,

God has a wonderful purpose for your people. He has always had that. Moreover, now that the time for the Lord's return draws closer, I hear the accelerating cry, *"Let My people go!!!"* I believe the remnant from the descendents of Ham is needed today more than at any other time in history. You were born to be warriors for God!

God's Blessing To All Noah's Children

In Genesis 9:1 we read, *"And God blessed Noah and his sons, and said to them, 'Be fruitful and multiply, and fill the earth.'"* That divine mandate is still very much alive. There is great blessing for your people if they take heed and do what is necessary to walk *"in the ways of the Lord."*

The following are historical examples of kings and nations who enjoyed God's blessings because they were in right relation with the children of Abraham. Remember the Lord's covenantal promise to Abraham: *"I will bless those who bless you..."* (Genesis 12:3)

Leaders & Nations Who Treated God's People Well

Pharoah, King of Egypt & Abimelech, one of the Philistine Kings

Both the Egyptians and Philistines were descended from Mizraim...all were Black. Though there were times when these nations were enemies of the Israelites, during Abraham's time, the kings of both nations <u>protected</u> him. You may recall the stories in Genesis 12 and 20 when Abraham and Sarah were passing through both countries. Abraham feared Sarah would be taken from him because of her beauty, so he lied and passed her off as his sister. Both times, God warned the kings and they released Sarah and spared Abraham's life. In the case of Abraham's sojourn in Gerar, King Abimelech befriended Abraham, and they remained friends throughout his life.

I love the account of Abraham's death in the Book of Jasher. He was buried in the cave of Ephron the Hittite, a descendant of Ham.

> *"When the inhabitants of Canaan* [descendants of Ham] *heard that Abraham was dead, they all came with their kings and princes and all their men to bury Abraham…all the inhabitants of the land wept on account of Abraham, for he had been good to them all, and because he had been upright with God and men. And there arose not a man who feared God like unto Abraham, for he had feared his God from his youth, and had served the Lord, and had gone in all his ways during his life, from his childhood to the day of his death. And the Lord was with him…and delivered him from the counsel of Nimrod and his people…and brought all the children of the earth to the service of God, and he taught them the ways of the Lord, and caused them to know the Lord…and the Lord God delivered the whole earth on account of Abraham."* [56] [Emphasis mine]

What an incredible story of the faithfulness of our patriarch, Abraham, and how God honored the descendents of Ham who were leaders in the earth and who treated Abraham and his descendents with reverence and high regard.

Egypt Under Joseph

You know this story well, Aleeyah…but just to review, God led young Joseph to experience slavery and hardship so that he would be raised up at the very time in history when the known world at that time was in danger. Through divine providence, and the dream interpretive gift of Joseph, Jacob's beloved son rose to the second highest rank of Vice-Regent in all of Egypt. Under Joseph [descendent of Shem], the nation founded by Mizraim [descendent of Ham] was saved. More than saved, Egypt flourished and was exceedingly blessed during this period in history.

Moses Made King Over Cush

There is a part of Moses' life that is not recorded in Scripture, but Jasher gives quite a lengthy account. This was the time period following the incident in Exodus 2 where Moses killed an Egyptian because he was beating a Hebrew slave, and hid the Egyptian in the sand. When they did not regard Moses as a "savior," Moses *"was afraid, and thought, 'Surely the thing is known.' When Pharoah heard of it, he sought to kill Moses."* (Exodus 2:14-15)

Moses left Egypt in haste, and because Scripture subsequently recounts Moses' time in Midian, we naturally assume he went straight from Egypt to Midian. Jasher, however, records an interim period of forty-nine years!

> *"Moses was eighteen years old when he fled from Egypt from the presence of Pharoah, and he escaped to the camp of Kikianus* [King of Cush]. *Moses was nine years in the camp of Kikianus King of Cush* [Ethiopia], *all the time that they* [Aram and the children of the East] *were besieging Cush, and Moses went out and came in with them. And the king and princes and all the fighting men loved Moses, for he was great and worthy, his stature was like a noble lion, his face was like the sun, and his strength was like that of a lion, and he was counselor to the king."* [57]

At the end of nine years with Moses risking his life for the people of Cush, King Kikianus fell ill and died. Guess whom the nation chose to rule over them? Moses. *"They stripped off each man his garments and cast them upon the ground, and they made a great heap and placed Moses thereon. And they rose up and blew with trumpets and called out before him, and said, 'May the king live...and they made Moses king over them on that day."* [58] Moses was twenty-seven when he became King of Cush, where he ruled for forty years!

> *"The Lord granted Moses favor and grace in the eyes of all the children of Cush, and they loved him exceedingly."* [59]* Once again, the descendants of Ham [Cush] placed a Semite [Moses] in a leadership position, and the entire nation enjoyed God's favor and blessing.

Aleeyah, lest you think God intends only Jews to rule and descendants of Ham to be servants, please observe that in each of the above instances, the rulers of each of these countries were Hamites [Pharoah, Abimelech and Kikianus], but God raised up Moses, Joseph and Abraham to bring God's favor to these nations and bless the people. It is this mutual regard by the descendants of Shem and Ham that the Lord is after...not the subjugation of your people.

---

* *Stephen, in Acts 7:23-40, says Moses spent 40 years with Egypt and 40 years away from Egypt. This appears to be a discrepancy. However, it is not if indeed Moses spent 18 years in Upper Egypt, then 49 years in Ethiopia [Lower Egypt], 12 years in Midian, then at 80 years old, he led the Egyptian Exodus.* [60]

Angelic Hosts Follow God's People

Angelic protection is one huge benefit of living under the Abrahamic covenant. Even though the Jews as a nation rejected Jesus as the Messiah, their rejection does not obviate God's covenant promise to His people. We in the United States often forget this.

There are some 13.3 million Jews in the world. 37% live in Israel. After Gibraltar [at the southern tip of Spain], which has 24%, the United States is third with 20%. God has favored and blessed our nation, not because we are anything special, but because we welcomed His children who fled during the Nazi occupation of Europe. We cared for and stood by them as a nation. We recognized God's blessing and destiny on their lives and celebrate their many achievements in the Arts and Sciences. When our country and its leaders no longer stand behind Israel, I believe we will witness an immediate open door to the enemy, leading to our own national demise.

By choosing to live under the Abrahamic covenant, this blessing extends to you and your children as well.

SUGGESTED PRAYER
"Holy Father, I humbly confess the wrong attitudes my ancestors may have had toward the descendents of Abraham, the people You chose to teach us Your ways. I ask You to forgive any disconnect in my spirit with regards to Israel, and to Jerusalem, where You will reign forever. I desire to dwell with my brothers and sisters of the faith in unity.

I choose by an act of my will to bind myself to the blessings of the covenant You made with Abraham, and Isaac, and Jacob, and to join myself to the godly root of my forefathers of the faith. Thank You for the purpose You have for me and my children. Restore us to be true warriors in the faith and to take our places of dominion that You foreordained. Let us stand strong in this evil day, bright shining as the sun. In the name of Jesus, amen."

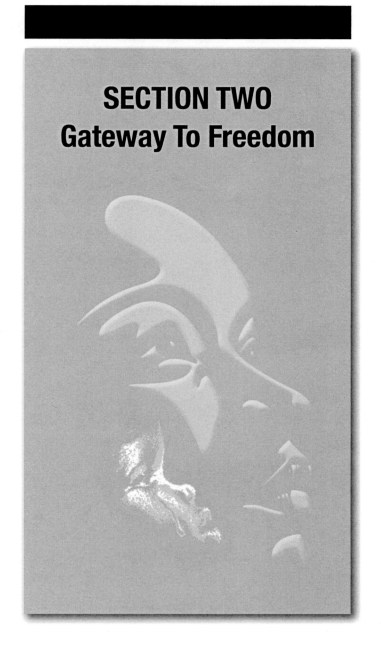

SECTION TWO
Gateway To Freedom

LETTER 13
The Blood Speaks

Dear Aleeyah,

Section Two is a very personal, introspective and interactive part of the book. Step by step you and I will take the journey into generational cleansing and inner healing. Please don't rush it, or feel like you have to finish a certain number of pages each day. Every step of this process, I have gone through. What awaits is incredible freedom. It's a realm of the Kingdom I never knew was possible. You may have gone through some of these things, but let's walk the journey together, so you can take others through it as well. Too many of God's women are not healed. The Father needs us in this incredible time in history.

The Blood Speaks

I want you to think about this statement for a moment. The blood <u>speaks</u>. With all the TV shows such as *Body of Proof, Bones,* and *CSI,* understanding the concept of a person's DNA speaking is not as foreign today as it was in biblical times.

In Genesis 4:10, the Lord tells Cain, *"The <u>voice</u> of your brother's blood cries to me from the ground, and from henceforth, <u>you are cursed</u> from the earth, which opened its mouth to receive your brother's blood from your hand."* [Emphasis added] The blood of our ancestors brings consequences, as we have seen in earlier chapters. You see from this verse alone that in Cain's case, shedding innocent blood brought about a divine curse.

In general, if our ancestors loved the Lord and followed His ways, there will be much blessing in our lives. The blessing is actually in the blood, because that's where the "life" is. If our ancestors worshipped <u>not</u> the Lord, that iniquity [i.e., inclination to sin] will land on us as a curse...down to the third and fourth generations. The "curse" is carried in our blood...and it will speak to us in countless ways.

As a "mother to many," you are responsible for spotting the fruit of any ancestral iniquity, both in your life and in the lives of your children. The Lord promises that He will hear every confession and prayer for cleansing...and your prayers carry the authority of Jesus. The confidence you have is that if there is a problem in one of your children that needs to be addressed, it **will** manifest. You will spot the fruit, and seek the root of that iniquity ...and help them pull it out. Throughout this section, I include common roots of iniquity that we all battle. I also offer suggested prayers as Holy Spirit may lead.

SUGGESTED PRAYER
"Holy Father, the greatest desire of my heart is to lay myself open and bare before You, and ask that You be gentle in Your dealing with me...Your daughter. You know the many wounds of my heart; and yet You said Your eye is always upon me. No matter where I am, You are here with me. Search me, O God, and create a new and right spirit within me. Transform me into the woman You created me to be. Bring to my remembrance anything that exalts itself against You. Circumcise my heart, that I would follow Your ways. You said a broken and contrite heart You would not despise...that when I draw near to You, You will draw near to me. Thank You for being with me, and for bringing up those things which need to be healed. In Jesus' name, amen."

List & Renounce The Ancestral Sins You Know About

Aleeyah, the first step is to list all the negative traits of the women in your family. Whether they were controlling, manipulative, cruel, whores, physically abusive, alcoholics, drug addicts, or whatever...I have found it very important to verbally confess my ancestors' sins and renounce them...speak them out.

Allow me to go a little deeper, though, for I have discovered that when it comes to His Levites – those whom He is preparing to serve Jesus when He returns – the Lord goes to the core, to cut out the deepest of bruises...perhaps even some you have no memory of. Remember, Levites have a different calling from "regular Christians." Just to reiterate, the principle is this: *all Israelites came out of Egypt, but not all of them were Levites. In the same way, all true believers are Christians and going to heaven, but not all of them are called into a levitical level of ministry before the Lord.*

This is not a "higher order" of Christianity; rather, a levitical calling is just that. It is a "calling." As in the Old Testament, the tribes were concerned primarily about their inheritance, their promised land. The Levites, on the other hand, were separated from the others and appointed by God Himself to care for those things that are His...His place of dominion in the earth. <u>He</u> was their inheritance, not "stuff." It's not that others of God's children don't care about Him. They do, but there's something different about being set apart and trained to "carry" those things that belong to the Lord. It is a calling involving one's priorities and focus. Today's Levites have a greater sensitivity to defilement, and they guard as precious their times with the Lord, rather than "hanging out" with friends like the rest of the people do.

One of the chief responsibilities of this new levitical breed is to "spot uncleanness" in others, and remove it. This involves spiritual disciplines of discernment, casting out demons and dismantling demonic strongholds. I believe you are so called, Aleeyah, and you understand what I'm talking about. But for the sake of your children who are also so called, help them to see that God requires from us a deeper cleansing...an antiseptic scrubbing of the soul, if you will...for He cannot dwell in the midst of defilement. This "scrubbing" can be painful.

An Example Of My Own DNA Cleansing

I have written much in *The Levitical Calling* about my admiration for a dear spiritual mentor, Elizabeth Hairston-McBurrows, Founder of Women With A Call International and The Apostolic-Prophetic Connection. One of my toughest DNA cleaning lessons involved a conference she was holding a few years ago in Atlanta.

To provide backstory: she had talked with me about a book on worship that she had been working on for years, and asked what it would take for me to help her with it. At the time, my ad agency was over 25 years old, and I had produced 14 books for clients. At this particular time, however, work was slow...and frankly, I needed the job. I quoted her what I thought was a fair price.

A Troubling Dream

The first night of the conference, I had a very disturbing dream. I was with my cousins in my grandmother's back yard. I looked down at my hands and arms and they were covered with boils...big pus-filled boils with squiggly blackhead-looking markings at the head. It was ugly. In the dream, I was very alarmed because this infestation was spreading, and I had no idea what it was or how to get rid of it. My cousins came over, took one look at my arms and said, *"Eeww....gross! Why do you have this and we don't?"* (a strange question) My answer in the dream was even stranger: *"Because I am the first issue of strength."* I woke up.

The dream troubled me all the way to the conference. Two things were clear:

1. There was something under my skin that was inherited, for the "squiggly" line was a DNA strand. I recognized it as such. Plus, when I answered, *"I am the first issue of strength,"* that is biblical language for *"first-born."* This meant that whatever was wrong with my ancestors...I had received the strongest concentration of it since I was the first-born.

2. Secondly, this thing was endangering me. It would spread unless I dealt with it.

I was uneasy throughout the meeting. A pastor was speaking, comparing Elisha's regard for and devotion to Elijah to that of the "school of the prophets" who just wanted to get from the great prophet whatever they could, but were unwilling to make any personal sacrifices on his behalf. She then referred to Dr. Elizabeth as our spiritual covering, and that we need to have the attitude of Elisha, willing to serve her.

Zap!

I couldn't get home fast enough. Though I didn't have long before the evening session, I was under deep conviction. I fell prostrate on the floor and asked the Lord to search my heart and rid me of this ancestral infestation. Holy Spirit began to illuminate what was under my skin...and it was despicable!

He finally spoke. He was gentle, not condemning...but what He said I will never forget. *"My child, when you grew up, you were the __served__...blacks were the __servants__. You need to repent for the prejudice in your maternal ancestral line. I have allowed it to surface so you will see it clearly. It is no accident that I brought you under one of My choicest servants as a spiritual covering, a black woman. I want __you__ to serve __her__ as unto __Me__."*

This was ancestral sin at its core...and the Lord wanted it purged from me. I cried tears of repentance and laid my ancestral prejudice, and the pride of entitlement, on the altar. He was pleased with my sacrifice, and the heavy burden of conviction lifted.

During the evening service, I sat behind Dr. Elizabeth. At the end, I leaned up and whispered, *"Get your manuscript ready...I want to help you with your book. There will be no charge...it will be my joy to help you."*

Tears ran down her cheeks. We worked on her book for months. I interviewed her and wove those personal stories into what the Lord has taught her concerning how to approach Him in worship and bring others into His presence. I would never have gotten to know this woman of God up close like this, unless I first learned to humble myself before Him by serving her. Her book, *The Wonder of Worship,* is a testament to the Lord's blessing both her and me. I made not one cent on the editing and production of the book that took months to complete...but I wouldn't trade anything for the wealth of wisdom I received.

The Poisonous Roots of Our Female Ancestors

You will notice that in the discussion about our patriarchs, not one woman was mentioned. We know, though, that when Jesus returns, He will have both men and women serving Him, for the mandate to exercise dominion that God gave in Genesis was to <u>both</u> Adam and Eve. Unfortunately, we do not have a long historical record of women who walked with God. Yes, we have Hannah, Sarah, Deborah, Esther and Ruth, among others...but compared to the list of godly men, the women pale in comparison.

I believe it will please the Lord immensely if you do all you can to instruct your daughters and granddaughters that purging defilement from their souls is an important levitical *key* to their growth as women of God. How much we need strong, godly black women for the days ahead!

The following are six of our collective female ancestral constructs (i.e., strongholds). They aren't pretty...but they are alive and well in every woman, and are actually part of our iniquitous bloodline as women. I encourage you and your children to come before the Lord and ask Him to reveal any places where you have been manifesting their behaviors.

Because this section is interactive – meaning, you read and then pray – please take your time with this. It is very important! One young Levite was so serious about cleansing herself that she focused on only one each day until she got through this chapter.

#1- JEZEBEL (The Controller)

This ancestor loves to manipulate people like pawns on a chessboard. She needs to create total dependency on her from those around her, and often triangulates one person against another. She'll say one thing to you in order to create the illusion of "closeness," only to turn around and say something bad about you to someone else with whom she needs to bond. She may throw a fit when her man doesn't do what he's supposed to do...then gloats with a martyr's pride that it's up to her to care for the entire family. They would all fall apart without her. If she starts to lose control over a situation, watch out. She will spend hours coming up with ways to turn the situation around to her favor. Rather than wait upon the Lord and give a situation to Him, the Jezebel DNA is compelled to manipulate the circumstances so she can get back in control. Her strategies are endless: she may be coy and flattering, but when that doesn't work, she morphs into a commandant! Jezebel is front and center in many of our churches and ministry groups. She finds it very difficult to submit to anyone else...convinced that the Lord has spoken and what He said to her far outweighs what He may have said to anyone else.

I once heard about a well-known ministry leader who took over the offering at a conference that was not hers, but one in which she was speaking. She announced, "Leave blank the 'Pay to the order of' part, and we'll fill them in later." The congregation, like sheep, obeyed because she was a so well known, thinking surely they could trust her. Her minions then followed the offering plate out of the sanctuary and subsequently bullied the lesser-experienced host, until they had gathered up every last check, and dollar bill before leaving town. The ministry host was left penniless. Jezebel had struck again.

SUGGESTED PRAYER
"Holy Father, I desire that when people look at me they would see Jesus. Toward that end, I renounce every conscious and subconscious participation with actions and behavior that are unbecoming a woman of God. I confess and renounce the iniquity of Jezebel [name those controlling and manipulative behaviors] *and loose myself from them. Thank you that when I confess my sins, You hear from heaven and cleanse me of all unrighteousness. In Jesus' name, amen."*

#2- DELILAH (The Seductress)

The name *Delilah* means "coquette and languishing"(i.e., appearing helpless). In our immoral, permissive culture, our churches are filled with Delilahs, and I would venture to say that it was Delilahs who seduced the fallen Watcher Angels. Enoch refers to them as "*sirens.*" A Delilah spirit seduces with her attire, with eyes that steal glances at a man in another pew...who sprinkles her conversations with helplessness or flattery, and often dishes out sexual favors. The actual Delilah gave herself over to a spirit of seduction, deceit, lies and betrayal.

In Judges 16:19 we read, "*She made him* [Samson] *sleep upon her knees.*" The word for "sleep" is *yashen* which means "to be slack or languid." This is a demonically-charged sexual lure that powerful men fall into time and time again. This is not a God-induced sleep...it is bewitching. Interestingly, the same word is used when God put Adam into a "deep sleep" – only in Samson's case, the enemy made him fall into a counterfeit of God's sleep.

This type of seduction is rampant in today's culture. I think of Governor Mark Sanford of South Carolina, who was so mesmerized by his South American "soul mate" that he willingly gave up his wife, family, career and reputation just to be with her. Every powerful governmental leader who has fallen (Bill Clinton, Gary Hart, Arnold Schwarzenegger, former Congressman Anthony Wiener) has encountered a woman with a Delilah spirit.

This spirit is archaic. We first see it in Genesis 6 that we have discussed at length; but as you read these verses again, I want you to imagine what these women were like, who were such easy prey for the fallen Watcher Angels.

"*And it came to pass, when men began to multiply on the face of the earth and daughters were born to them, that the sons of God* [i.e., fallen angels] *saw that the daughters of men were fair; so they took them wives of all whom they chose... There were giants on the earth in those days; and also after that, for the sons of God came in unto the daughters of men, and they bore children to them, and they became giants who in the olden days were mighty men of renown.*" (Genesis 6:1-4)

I do not believe that these "daughters of men," were innocent victims of demonic perversion. I believe these women *seduced* the fallen angels! They were actual participants in this atrocity against humanity. A full description of their siren-like behavior is found in *The Lost Book of Enoch*, and *The Secrets of Enoch* from *The Forgotten Books of Eden*. The fallen angels were huge, strong and handsome. More than that, they possessed secret powers and promised to share this hidden knowledge with the women: various potions to draw people to them, or how to cast spells on ones they were angry with. Such knowledge of being able to control others was extremely seductive.

These beings taught them to manufacture dyes and create flashy clothing...how to adorn their eyes with pigments – all to appear more alluring to unsuspecting males that were the targets of their or their daughters' affections. Yes, the Watchers lured these women with witchcraft-type power that God forbade His children from embracing. Plus, these women knew that by having sex with them, their children would be bigger and "badder" than every other kid in the neighborhood.

Whenever a woman "feigns" or "pretends" any sort of behavior (helpless, needy, flirtatious, pretending to be interested because of what she might get from him), the actions find their root in the guile and deceit of the Delilah spirit. With these women, there always seems to be an "agenda." In Delilah's case, her true motivation was *"thirteen hundred pieces of silver"* from every Philistine lord. (Judges 16:5) Jesus commended Nathaniel, as one in whom *"there is no guile."* (John 1:47) The Lord desires His women to be without guile too. We need to loose ourselves from the Delilah spirit in our ancestry.

SUGGESTED PRAYER
"Father, I desire only to seek You, not someone to replace You. Search my heart and reveal the seductive behaviors in my life and in the lives of my ancestors. I confess the iniquity of Delilah [name the seductive behaviors]. I renounce these sins and ask You to cleanse me of all unrighteousness. Thank You, Lord, for Your gift of mercy and forgiveness. In Jesus' name, amen."

#3- ATHALIAH (The Emasculator)

This woman was King Ahab's sister. Their father was Omri, who was King of Israel, and notoriously evil. They were used to being in power. What we know about this woman is that after Athaliah's son Ahaziah reigned as king for one year, he was killed by divine determination because he was wicked. (2 Chronicles 22:7) Verse 10 says *"When Athaliah the mother of Ahaziah saw that her son was dead, she arose and destroyed all the king's sons of the house of Judah."* She was completely wicked, and had it not been for her sister rescuing young Joash, she would have killed him too.

A woman with an Athaliah spirit has little regard for the leadership destiny of the men in her family. She takes every opportunity to minimize them, put them down, mock them or make fun of how useless they are. This is a very subtle spirit...for it can manifest in many a church. With God calling women to serve Him in these days, it is easy for a woman to conclude – even subconsciously – that He is displeased with men who just sit in the pew to please their wives, but who manifest little zeal for the Lord. It is easy for a woman to look down her spiritual nose at her husband...and decide to "help God out" and take over the ministry herself. This surely does not please the Lord.

This spirit operated strongly in my family and I have spent much time repenting for it. I believe there <u>is</u> a reason why God is calling women today...but it is <u>not</u> to take over the foreordained place of men.

Not long ago, I was reading Jeremiah and fell under deep conviction.

"Thus says the Lord: If they can break my ordinances of the day, and my ordinances of the night, so that there should not be day and night in their appointed time; Then may also my covenant which I made with David my servant be broken, so that he should not have an heir to reign upon his throne and my covenant with the priests and the Levites, my ministers..." (Jeremiah 33:20-21)

"Priests...Levites...ministers..." These were <u>men</u>, not women! God made a covenant with David that He will <u>always</u> have men to serve Him as priests and ministers and Levites! He did not decree that men would flake out and not come to their assignment...and God would then have to give that assignment to women. No! God has a pre-ordained position of ministerial leadership for His men! It is His plumb line covenant with them. As women, we should long for them to take their places, and pray expectantly for them to come forth!

When Holy Spirit's conviction hit me, I prayed, *"Father, I confess and renounce the emasculating spirit of my ancestors,"* then began to pray earnestly for God's MEN to arise. I know many women who are strong leaders in ministry...some much stronger than their husbands. The last thing I want to do is convey to readers that God's levitical army in the end times will be made up of mostly women. The Lord needs both men and women to serve Him. We have two unique assignments and are foreordained to work together in unity and to extend mutual regard for one another regarding our respective callings.

> SUGGESTED PRAYER
> *"Lord, search me and know my thoughts, and conform me to the proper regard for the males in my family. Let my speech be flavored with encouragement. I confess the iniquity of Athaliah* [name the negative attitudes you have harbored and any critical words spoken against your husband, sons, father, and any other male figure in your life]. *Let my heart be filled with your love and understanding as they become all that You ordained them to be. In Jesus' name, amen."*

#4- EVE (The Deceiver)

The mother of us all opened a floodgate that fights to hold us bondage day in and day out. Her great sin was that she assumed she knew what God had said...that she could actually hold court with the enemy of our souls and prevail...that the feelings of delight she experienced when she saw the fruit of the forbidden tree were so strong that reason or a simple "check in her spirit" was not on her radar...that then she could pull her husband into complicity by batting her eyelashes!

The Lord decreed Eve's punishment: *"To the woman he said, 'I will greatly multiply your pain and your conception; in pain you shall bring forth children, and you shall be dependent on your husband, and he shall rule over you.'"* (Genesis 3:16, Lamsa's translation from the Aramaic of the Peshitta) In other translations, it reads, *"Your desire shall be for your husband."* The word "desire" is *teshuwquah* and it means "to run after, chase, be desperate for." It is the same Hebrew word that is used in Genesis 4:7 as the Lord speaks to Cain saying, *"Sin lies at the door. Its desire is for you..."* Sin desired to run after and rule over Cain, in the same way that woman's desire is to run after and rule over her husband. Every married woman knows what a curse this is! Deep in our hearts we want our man to be the leader...but the reality of the Fall remains: Woman's "default" programming is **domination**...man's "default" is **passivity**. God help us!

SUGGESTED PRAYER

"Holy Father, I desire that when others look at me they would see Jesus. Toward that end, I renounce every conscious and subconscious participation with actions and behavior that are unbecoming a woman of God. I confess the iniquity of Eve, the sinful desire in my heart to dominate and control my husband, and [name any deceitful behaviors]. *I ask You to be mindful of Your promise that when I confess my sins, You hear my sins and cleanse me of my unrighteousness. Thank You, Lord, for Your mercy and Your incredible sacrifice for my sins. Amen."*

#5- THE RELIGIOUS WOMAN

This woman is perhaps more difficult to spot than all the others. She is not overtly evil, for she has a deep desire to love and follow the Lord. But just because a woman is a religious leader doesn't mean that her theologies, doctrines and behaviors are biblical. We must be careful whom we emulate. Ironically, since I had been basically non-churched most of my life, it was this Religious Woman the Lord used to show me an important key to gender transformation.

When a male ministry colleague back in 1971 told me that he neither liked me nor respected me as a woman, it prompted an all-night vigil with the Lord. This man verbally attacked the core of who I was as a woman. Only two years old as a believer, I had to know why I [or he] was not seeing the promised transformation as a result of being born again. *What was I doing wrong?*

What the Lord taught me that night is that I had created a "stereotype" of a Christian woman. She was nothing like me. In my view, a "woman of God" was syrupy, nauseatingly sweet, and told cutesy little stories at Bible studies that made me want to gag. She was not dynamic, nor particularly gifted...she taught the Bible in nice proper homes filled with nice proper ladies – all white with coiffed bobbed hairdos. None of that was me, except the "white" part! Back then, I was more akin to a Women's Libber.

My Personal Turnaround

During my vigil, I listed all the qualities of this phantom "woman of God," and concluded that because I wasn't anything like that, God was forced to take what I was and start from there. Not wise to force the Almighty into an entirely new "doctrine!"

What He asked me to do next was radical. He said, *"Look up all the verses about My women, and list their qualities."* I did. What I found was that those qualities were ones I didn't object to at all. I desired to have a gentle and quiet spirit...have a heart my husband could safely trust in...be so secure in who I was that I could trust God to lead through my husband...have wisdom and discernment to make the right decisions for my family...be able to step out in bold business ventures all my own, encouraged by my husband, and have the faith that whatever was in my hand would be more than enough venture capital...be able to exercise every spiritual gift He gave me. None of these were sappy qualities.

Then and there, about five in the morning, I made a covenant with the Lord. Looking at the three lists I had made, I prayed something like this:

"Lord, here's the list that describes me as I am now...here's my stereotype of the Christian woman [which I hated]*...but here's this one over here of what You would like for me to be. So okay, I lay down all that I am right now, rough edges and all... and choose to trust that You will somehow turn me into this list over here. There is no way that I can do it...but since I know I am praying according to Your will, I choose to believe that You will."*

That was it. There were no goose bumps...no drum rolls...but there was an act of my will to lay down all I was and trust Him to make me <u>His</u> woman. Within two weeks, transformation became noticeable...and I have been transforming ever since.

SUGGESTED PRAYER

First, make your own lists...and use the above prayer as a guide, if you like. The important thing to realize is that He will answer a heartfelt prayer. *"This is the confidence that we have in Him, that if we ask anything according to His will, He hears us: For if we beseech Him to hear us concerning the things that we ask of Him, <u>we are assured that we have already received from Him those things that we desire</u>."* (I John 5:14-15, Lamsa's translation of the Aramaic Peshitta) [Emphasis mine]

#6- THE VICTIM

This category of women is different from the others, but I feel impressed to include her. She is not an actual person such as Eve, Jezebel, or Delilah...but she is alive nonetheless, and we need freedom from her, too.

Many women have been physically abused, sexually abused or molested when children. These experiences wreak havoc in a young girl's psyche, and she can easily develop a victim mentality, feeling as if somehow she was to blame for it and doesn't deserve any better treatment. Such a woman will often go from man to man, experiencing a string of abusers...almost as if she desires or expects to attract them.

I have ministered to many such victims, and their stories break my heart. One of my spiritual daughters was "sold" by her mother to the family priest at age 5. The deal was this: the priest would bring food for the family, and while there, the mother was to leave her little daughter alone with him to do whatever sick thing he wanted to do to her. Woeful are the curses that befall such a mother...and such a "priest!"

Remember How Defilement Operates

The principle of how defilement works, when properly understood, brings tremendous freedom. Thus, Aleeyah, if you or your children have been sexually abused, please teach them this principle.

God requires us to be without blemish, to be "undefiled." What is a "blemish?" The Hebrew word is *tamiym* (pronounced taw-meem) which means "entire" in a literal, figurative or moral sense. The word has the meaning of "entire soundness, integrity, truth, clean, complete." That is God's standard for us. The word *tamiym* contains the Hebrew root *muwm* meaning "to stain" or "to blemish."

When you see a bruise on a piece of fruit, what do you do? You take a knife and cut it out. As it relates to our lives, a "bruise" is that "thing" or incident wherein we were stained [i.e., defiled]. It is that place of defilement that must be removed. After all, God desires truth in the inner being. Entire truth.

The concept of "stain" and "blemish," therefore, is both a verb that refers to the action of defiling someone...as well as a noun that is the visible <u>mark</u> (i.e., bruise) left behind from that stain. Remember, part of a Levite's calling is to "spot the bruises" in another in order to bring healing to them.

The Abusive Cycle

When a young girl has been abused, the action [sexual or otherwise] of the abuser leaves a "stain" or "blemish" in her soul...through no fault of her own. I don't care if she felt pleasurable things while the abuse was going on. That is simply bodily response, which we were created by the Creator to feel! It is critical to communicate this to young women, because the enemy loves to destroy our self-images as women.

What the enemy does is speak lies to the young girl's mind saying, *"This was your fault...you seduced him...there is badness in you, because you know it felt good!"* Then the young girl carries around these voices in her head, as well as the bruises in her soul without knowing how to cleanse herself from them. What is happening is that she actually "carries" or "manifests" the perverse spirit that defiled her.

In an earlier chapter, we discussed the intent of an evil spirit: he looks for anyone in whom he can make his home. What happens is that when that young, innocent but bruised girl is around others, a predator who operates freely in an immoral or perverse spirit "recognizes" the spirit that has bruised the girl. He then heads for her like a magnet. It is evil spirit that seeks to attach to another evil spirit, thereby strengthening the so-called "molecular power" of the stronghold of immorality.

Keep in mind that this evil spirit is <u>not</u> the girl. Rather, the spirit of the person who abused her **attached** to [or "bonded with"] her. If there were an open door of iniquity in her ancestral bloodline, it had a legal right to mess with her. The sad reality is that without proper deliverance and healing, she can carry that "familiar spirit" throughout life and continue to attract creepy men.

This is Satan's strategy: *defile us or stain us, and thereby render us ineffective for the Lord.* Over many years of ministry, I have observed that those who experience the greatest defilement when young have the greatest calling on their lives. The enemy knows when a child carries a strong anointing. Thus, he targets us as children, hoping to warp us up with so many "blemishes" that we will be derailed in our development as ministers of the Lord Most High.

SUGGESTED PRAYER

"Father in heaven, there is no way I can change in and of myself. I can only ask You to be true to Your promise that through the redemptive power of Holy Spirit, You will transform my inner heart. I look to You to lead me beside the still waters of Your Presence. Heal me, Lord...

LETTER 14
The Keys Of Binding & Loosing

Dear Aleeyah,

Before we go any deeper, understanding the meaning of the words *binding* and *loosing* is an important key to our healing. We all know that through Jesus, we are given authority to *bind* and *loose*. But what does this really mean? We go about *binding* the evil one...but what do we really *loose*?

The word *bind* is *deo*. It means "to tie in bonds or wind in bonds." To *loose* is *luo*, which means "to loosen, break up, or dissolve." This word *loose* doesn't just shatter something... rather, the verb reduces a thing to the constituent particles. In other words, it completely obliterates something into the atomic, unseen particles from which it was constructed in the first place! The authority the Savior gives us obliterates a spiritual stronghold to such a degree that it will never be re-constructed again!

Let me give you an example.

One unspoken message I received from my female ancestors was, *"You can't trust men. They are weak, and you will have to do everything yourself if you want anything done."* Once I tracked down the lie, confessed and renounced the stronghold [i.e., mental construct], then Jesus gave me the authority to loose myself from that thing and obliterate it...sort of like nuking the lie with a laser gun! An example of such a prayer might be:

"Lord, I <u>loose</u> myself from the lie that men are weak and not dependable, and <u>bind</u> myself by an act of my will to the truth of Your Word for these men, that they will grow in righteousness, walk worthy of Your calling, and that my husband would regard me as a true helpmeet, a woman who loves You and desires to serve You with all my heart. Amen." [Note: This prayer can be used to cancel other lies as well.]

Once you *loose* yourself from something, though, you have to *bind* yourself to something else, because you're out there naked, so to speak! In my case, over the years I had bound myself to a lie that consistently messed up relationships with the men in my life. Once the realization came, I *loosed* myself from the lie and *bound* myself to the Word of God that declares that men are created in the image of God. They are uniquely marked for leadership and righteousness. There is now no enmity between male and female according to His Word.

The Plumb Line

God has a plumb line when it comes to His levitical women. He wants people to look at us and see Jesus. Period. As culture, ancestral iniquity and soulish wounding cause our demeanor and behaviors to be skewed toward worldliness, that doesn't mean that God has changed. On the contrary, it just means that we have further to go in being transformed.

The Hebrew word for *plumb line* is *anak*, a root word that means "to be narrow." God's way is always narrow. We don't change theology regarding how women of God are to act any more than we can change the theology on sexual orientation by saying that God makes some people gay!

SUGGESTED PRAYER
"Lord Jesus, You promised that whatever I <u>loose</u> in Your name is loosed in heaven, and the very act of loosing totally obliterates those things that I have consciously or unconsciously bound myself to. I <u>loose</u> myself from every false agreement I have made with my mother and all female ancestors. I <u>loose</u> myself from Jezebel, from Delilah, from Athaliah, and from Eve. I <u>loose</u> myself from coming into agreement with a wounded personality and construct of behaviors that do not reflect You. I <u>bind</u> myself to the woman You created me to be: a woman with a gentle and quiet spirit, a woman whose husband safely trusts in her. [If you are married] I desire my husband's highest good. I desire that You bring him to his fullest expression of giftedness and leadership. I release him to You...trusting that You are my ultimate Protector, and that You will show me how to walk faithfully through the difficult times. Help me to love him as he deserves. Help me experience release and freedom in being a wife and mother. Help me to cast every care and expectation on You. I love You, Lord. Amen."

LETTER 15
The Need For Generational Cleansing

Dear Aleeyah,

As you grow in your ministry calling, you will also grow in learning to recognize bruises of the heart, both in yourself and in your children. An important clue to spotting them lies in specific patterns of behavior that trigger a wrong or ungodly response over and over again.

Consider some examples:

#1 After a painful divorce, I began dating my childhood sweetheart. In the early months of our courtship, my emotions were a roller coaster. One minute I was drawn to Mike. The next minute, I wanted to run from him as far away as I could. The "desire to run away" became a troubling behavioral response that I was powerless to control. Poor Mike. He never knew from one day to the next what I would be feeling toward him. It took months for me to even get up the courage to discuss it, for I did not want to hurt his feelings and admit that sometimes I had no feelings for him at all...and worse, wanted to run away from him. I knew the problem was clearly mine. My fear, of course, was that the pain of having been rejected by my first husband was so deep that I had somehow become an emotional cripple. To say I agonized before the Lord is an understatement. There was clearly a blockage that prevented me from getting on with my life and embracing Mike's love for me, as well as God's freedom for me as a woman.

It was at this juncture where I had to make a choice: Will I repress the "fear of what I might discover" and blunder on through life half-alive? Or, will I submit to the searchlight of the Spirit of God to fully reveal the core of the bruise?

Often, that excision requires professional help.

I decided to confront whatever it was and deal with it. I'll never forget Mike and I sitting in our counselor's office. Dr. Parsons is a Christian psychologist and very skilled at her work. She asked me to explain earlier memories in my life when I experienced this "desire to run away." A memory or two began to surface, and I described them. Then, she asked me to close my eyes and <u>ask</u> to see the earliest memory of this emotional behavior.

Within seconds, I burst into an avalanche of sobs. Normally very "together," I came unglued in front of her, and in front of Mike. I was crying so hard that I couldn't breathe. Needless to say, the Lord was revealing the core, the root, of this bruise. I share this very personal memory because I want you to know, Aleeyah, that we **all** have deep hurts, and we should not be ashamed to explore them and expunge them from our being.

The image I *saw* was my mother and I sitting on a couch. When I was finally able to speak, I explained that my mother was an alcoholic...and for much of my life I, as a child, sat next to her on the living room couch trying to console her in her drunken state. I was trying to <u>*fix*</u> my mother and make her stop crying, but she was sucking the life out of me. That "feeling of wanting to flee" was very real. This deep *bruise* was now manifesting in my present relationship with Mike. The subconscious part of me was terrified that I would no longer have control over my life...that he would get too close and suck the life out of me just like my mother had done. I couldn't risk opening myself up again.

The bruise began to be excised that day. What was needed was for me to acknowledge that inner pain...recognize fully where it came from...and forgive my mother for not being the emotionally whole woman I needed as a young child. After undergoing this excision, I am now able to spot a behavioral pattern that taps into this old root, and bring every thought and feeling captive to the obedience of Christ. (2 Corinthians 10:5) By God's grace, I am no longer beset by this particular behavior.

Because I was not fully developed as a *child*, I can easily spot this condition in others. That's why it's so important that Levites take the initiative to undergo Holy Spirit examination. We must have our own bruises cut out, so that we can help others. And like Dr. Parsons, there are many who are uniquely gifted and called to perform such examinations. These are your pastors, counselors, deliverance ministers and "regular folks" who function in these giftings.

#2 I got to know Shirley (not her real name) several years ago. A pastor and strong woman of God, I listened to her angst when she started dating again after the death of her husband. As a widow myself, I understood where she was coming from. I could clearly see that a part of her was missing, and I began to explore her life as a child.

Born into a family of slaves, Shirley told me about picking cotton as a child. As the eldest daughter, she was left with the responsibility of taking care of her siblings. I knew immediately the source of her *bruise*. She had stuffed that "little girl" so far down inside her that she was not capable of appearing "vulnerable" and "needy." She had to be *in control* at all times. I understood the symptoms. I had them too.

I began to tell Shirley my story and asked, *"If you were to show me a picture of you when you think of yourself as a little child, describe that picture to me?"* She was a deer in headlights. She had no conscious memory of that young child. That's because the *child* no longer existed for her.

A year before, I went to an art show in Denver and saw the award-winning pencil drawing by a gifted New York artist, Jeanette Martone. It brought me to tears. I was so moved, in fact, that I took a photo of the drawing. At my next meeting with Shirley, I brought a copy of the picture and said, *"Is this how you felt as a child?"* Her eyes filled with tears. I gave her the photo and encouraged her to use it as a visual portrait of her "inner child" and talk to her, since she was

Pencil drawing by New York artist, Jeanette Martone. Used by permission.

still a living, vital part of her. I said, *"Welcome her, and all her conflicted feelings, into your life and give her the freedom to express all the sorrow she was never allowed to as a child."*

Shirley's Transformation

I don't know when I have ever seen such a powerful transformation. Shirley wrote me some weeks later, overjoyed that she had made peace with her *little girl*, and was now able to love again. She married six months later...and wrote that the "healing of that little girl part of her" finally released her be the woman God intended her to be.

Jesus said, *"Unless you turn and become like children, you will never enter the Kingdom of heaven."* (Matthew 18: 3) What's amazing is that the expression "become like children" is the Greek word for "convert." If I'm not mistaken, this is the only time the word *convert* is used in Scripture. And even more revealing, our *conversion* is not referring to becoming a Christian. It refers to becoming a <u>child</u> again!

Aleeyah, this is radical! What Jesus is saying is that it is the <u>child</u> part of us that needs to be set free. *"Where the Spirit of the Lord is, there is freedom."* (2 Corinthians 3:17) What Shirley did was allow the Spirit to release her little girl from bondage and be integrated into her Adult self. Glory to God!

To this day, I have a picture of me about 5 years old – playing dress up – framed and mounted in a prominent place in my bedroom. My *child* is always with me. I found tremendous freedom when I allowed her to express herself fully in my life.

My prayer is that this section will be helpful to you or your daughters who may have been likewise wounded.

The Power of God's Law

Part of the levitical calling is to explain why certain things keep happening to people. For example, there is a Proverb that says, *"A curse that is causeless does not light."* (Proverbs 26:2) The contrary is also true: *a curse that **has** cause* [i.e., legal right] **will** *light, or come upon the person.* This means that when a person's life, family, business, etc. is being destroyed by illness, catastrophe and/or financial ruin, the admonition to the Levite is to search for the open door through which the enemy had access. In other words, what about that person's life was left unattended and therefore vulnerable? Sure, bad things DO happen to God's people...but sometimes there is an underlying reason, and a Levite's duty is to search it out, instruct the person how to repent and close the door, and then align herself with walking in the ways of the Lord.

God's Word is _always_ true, regardless of a person's religion or understanding of Scripture. That is why the levitical calling is so critical: one of our duties is to keep the wrath of God from coming upon the people. You may ask, *"What is the wrath of God?"* It is a list of curses that God gave to Moses thousands of years ago, found in Deuteronomy 27 – 30. They could not be any more visible. In fact, God posted them on Mount Ebal for all to hear. These curses still live today. A Levite must be trained to spot them, and cleanse God's children from the wrath that will follow if not attended to.

A Levite In Training

I went to Nashville for a recording session and stayed with dear friends of mine. At dinner, I shared my journey regarding prophetic dreams. Ann (not her real name) said, *"I'd like to talk with you about my dreams; I have them all the time."* Then she added, almost under her breath, *"They are always in black and white."*

I said we would discuss it in the morning. I put her off because my inner beacon alerted me that something was wrong. After years studying the Hebraic method of interpreting dreams, I have learned that dreams in black and white typically are from the enemy. Therefore, I wanted to bring the matter before the Lord and ask for His counsel.

I looked through the bookshelves in the guest room as part of my "levitical examination." What I found supported my red flag. There were many New Age books on psychic experiences, reincarnation, the power of meditation, etc. I prayed and asked the Lord to guide me in helping Ann.

As the two of us sipped coffee the next morning, I asked, *"Ann, were you involved in the occult?"*

She replied, *"Yes, I was. How did you know? I used ouija boards and visited psychics. But I don't do that any more, of course, once I gave my life to Jesus."*

I said, *"But when you did this, you opened a door to the enemy and he now has a 'legal right' to come into your soul* [i.e., mind, will and emotions] *and try to destroy you, rob you of your sleep, and bring illnesses upon you."* I knew that she had struggled with health issues.

Alarmed, she asked, *"What do I do? I've never heard this teaching!"*

"We need to close the door."

I laid my hands on her and asked her to renounce her involvement with the occult and declare her total submission to Jesus Christ. I asked her to thank God, reminding her that *"When we confess our sins* [i.e., name them specifically] *He will forgive our sins and cleanse us from all unrighteousness."* (I John 1:9) I then commanded the spirits of deception, idolatry and disobedience to come out of her in the name of Jesus and blessed her in the name of the Father, the Son and Holy Spirit.

When I was driving back home, the Lord whispered, *"Your work is not done...there is still an open door."* As soon as He said this, I knew immediately what it was. I called Ann and said there was one thing more she needed to do. She responded immediately, *"I know...God showed me too...it's the books. What do I do with them?"*

I counseled her to put them all in a garbage bag and throw them away, along with every object (i.e., artifacts, crystals, charms, etc.) that demons can attach to, and to follow up with me in a few days. When we spoke later that week, she was totally joyous, *"I can't believe it...it's like something lifted off of me. And, I don't hear the voices anymore."*

I asked, *"What voices?"*

She replied, *"I've heard voices most of my life and assumed they were me. Now I know they were not. I'm really free!"* So free, as a matter of fact, that she has been helping others see the dangers of the occult and how we really **do** have authority to cast out evil spirits.

The Biblical Case For Ancestral Examination

There is still this issue with our ancestors...for *"the Lord visits the iniquity of the fathers upon the children to the third and fourth generation of those who hate Him."* (Exodus 20:5) Many Christians believe that once you ask Jesus into your life, you are automatically cleansed from every ancestral iniquity...so there is no need to go back over what people you never knew anyway did.

Jesus' death on the cross for our sins does not automatically obviate a person's need for confession of ancestral sins, for we must each bring our bloodline iniquities before the Father, and place them under the blood of Jesus. There is no magic eraser...rather, we are to lay ourselves *"open to the eyes of him with whom we have to do."* (Hebrews 4:13)

The Scriptures offer many examples to show how one generation confesses and repents for the sins of their fathers. The book of Deuteronomy is a beautiful example of Moses laying out the sins of the fathers...then the people collectively confessed them and asked forgiveness. This was necessary before they could enter their land of promise.

Later on in Jewish history, we read of Jews in one generation repenting for their forefathers' iniquity. For example, the prophet Daniel poured out his heart on behalf of his people. Jerusalem had just been destroyed and the Jews were scattered all over. In fact, Daniel himself was captured and taken to Babylon. These events were fresh on his mind. Confessing the sins of the fathers, he prayed,

> *"...the curse and oath which are written in the law of Moses the servant of God have been poured out upon us, because we have sinned against Him...He has confirmed his words...by bringing upon us a great calamity; for under the whole heaven there has not been done the like of what has been done against Jerusalem...because for our sins, and for the iniquities of our fathers, Jerusalem and thy people have become a byword among all who are round about us. O Lord, incline Thy ear and hear...for we do not present our supplications before thee on the ground of our righteousness, but on the ground of thy great mercy."* (Daniel 9:11-17) [Emphasis mine]

Other examples are found in Leviticus 26:40; Ezra's prayer in Nehemiah 9; and of course, the oft-quoted passage in 2 Chronicles 7:14, *"If my people who are called by my name humble themselves, and pray and seek my face, and turn from their wicked ways, then I will hear from heaven, and will forgive their sin and heal their land."*

This Practice Modeled By Jews Today

When attending synagogues during the High Holy Days, one of the most meaningful parts of these traditional Jewish services, for me, is asking forgiveness for the sins of our fathers. It is sad that a spiritual discipline, depicted and encouraged in Scripture, as well as modeled in Jewish synagogues today, is rarely discussed in churches.

Discovering My Own Open Door

I have followed the Lord with all my heart and soul since 1969. In all these years, I never went through a falling away or a time of willful disobedience. Notwithstanding, I would reach a certain point in my life and career when breakthrough seemed imminent, yet time after time I ended up helplessly watching everything fall apart.

Once, I found myself in a meeting in Nashville with three influential men in the music business: a manager, a record producer, and a booking agent. They were committed to my career and believed doors would soon open for a contract with a major label. What made the meeting more significant to me was the fact that I did absolutely <u>nothing</u> to instigate it. I thought, *"This is it, Lord. This is what You've been preparing me for!"* Within a month, the whole thing fell apart. Every door shut...record labels were only interested in signing well-known Christians like Kathie Lee Johnson (now Kathie Lee Gifford)...not an unknown like me.

Countless events such as this happened, the worst being the devastation caused by my theatrical musical's premiere on September 11, 2001. Not only was my production company in shambles, but personally I was left financially devastated, with no money to even buy groceries. It was as if a giant vacuum cleaner swept through my life and sucked up every seed of promised harvest.

For the next three years, I sought God. *Why did this happen? Do I have hidden unconfessed sin?* I searched Scripture for answers, and cried out, *"Lord, I am not leaving Your presence until You show me what is wrong."*

He always answers the cries of His children.

One day I was visiting an Atlanta church and perused its bookstore. My eyes locked onto a title, <u>Free From Freemasonry</u> by Ron G. Campbell. I bought the book knowing that a friend of mine had been involved in Masonry, along with her husband...and they had suffered difficult times. In fact, her husband died at a very young age, cutting short the ministry they had together.

I had "heard" that Masonry was dangerous but had no real understanding as to why. So, like a good little Levite, I began to read the book for <u>her</u>, not for me. Suddenly, I almost came off the couch reading the chapter called *"Understanding Generational Curses"* and the list of "curses" that often impact family members whose ancestors were involved in Masonry (taken from Deuteronomy 28). To my surprise, my family and I had experienced almost <u>every</u> curse.

The list includes:
- Mental and emotional problems
- Repeated or chronic sickness
- Barrenness, a tendency to miscarry or related female problems
- Breakdown of marriage
- Family alienation
- Premature deaths in the family
- Continued financial insufficiency[61]

I called my only living maternal aunt and asked if we had any Masons in our family. She said her father - my grandfather who died at age 37 - was a Shriner (one of the highest orders within Freemasonry). I then called about my father's side of the family. Lo and behold, I discovered Masonry there as well. As it turned out, I am a 3rd generation descendant of a Mason on both sides of my family!

I read the book again, to learn what made this organization so dangerous to so many good people…for I know that many Masons were involved in the founding of our nation. I learned that the majority of Masons join because they sincerely want to be of help to our country and to their communities, and likely do not understand the meaning of the vows they take in secret…which are, in actuality, vows to a false god. Just recently I learned that those who get to the seventh degree of Masonry (Royal Arch Degree) learn that the secret name of the Masonic deity is *Jaobulon* or *Jao-Bul-On.*[62]

Finding this book was a God-thing…for He began to show me that my ancestors' disobedience in making vows to a false deity had opened a legal door for the enemy to destroy my life. The Torah states very clearly, *"You shall not bow down to them* [false gods] *or serve them; for I the Lord your God am a jealous God, visiting the iniquity of the fathers upon the children to the third and the fourth generation of those who hate me…"* (Exodus 20:5)

The result of my study and subsequent enlightenment is that I repented for the sins of my forefathers and broke ties with all generational curses that may have come on my life either knowingly or unknowingly by my ancestors. I performed "identificational repentance" as is modeled in Leviticus 26:40, Nehemiah 9 and Daniel 9, and include a sample Prayer of Release. (See Appendix)

The results were dramatic. I began to experience the favor of God as never before. It was very real...as if an invisible "dark cloud" that had hung over my head were suddenly removed. My walk with the Lord deepened...the financial curse was broken off...I began to receive increased revelation from the Lord...and new music began to flood into this composer's soul.

Again, let me reiterate that generational curses are able to manifest in our family line whether we know anything about our ancestors or not. An "operational curse" means that the enemy has some legal right to freely mess with your life. Levites who operate in spiritual disciplines of ministry learn to spot evidence of such a curse over time.

The Curse Associated With Illegitimacy

I have learned much about breaking curses through my pastor and mentor, Pastor Sandy Mathis, founder of Georgia-based Sandy Mathis Ministries. Pastor Sandy has been a deliverance minister since the mid 80's and demonstrates a powerful anointing for breaking demonic strongholds, especially ones that are rooted in a curse.

In working with countless people in their attempts to "cut out the bruises," Pastor Sandy has seen remarkable results when the person repents for the sin of illegitimacy that is in his or her family line. This doesn't mean, for example, that you were illegitimate, or that you conceived a child out of wedlock. Rather, it refers to anyone in your ancestral line.

The Word of God says, *"No bastard shall enter the assembly of the Lord; even to the tenth generation none of his descendants shall enter the assembly of the Lord."* (Deuteronomy 23:2) The word *bastard* is the Hebrew word *mamzer*, which means "to alienate, a mongrel, i.e., born of a Jewish father and a heathen mother." [63]

I want to stress that God loves all his children. None of us is a mistake. And there is likely none of us whose family lineage does not have illegitimacy in it somewhere down the line. There were those in the messianic lineage, for example, who did not have the purest lineage. Think Rahab the harlot. What we are talking about here is that when there has been willful disregard for purity and holiness in matrimonial covenant relationship between a man and a woman, the enemy has "legal right" to mess up the lives of descendants of that line. I have included in the Appendix a Prayer of Release written by Pastor Sandy Mathis that I encourage you to pray. When we pray it sincerely, we are released from the consequences of this curse.

Don't Be A Curse Inspector

We are not to walk around worrying whether we have some curse operating in our lives. Believe me, if you have one, you will know it very plainly. There is no guessing game where the Word of God is concerned. There **will** be a physical or emotional manifestation of a "bruise." You or others will clearly see it.

Don't be too hard on yourselves if you see a manifestation. On the contrary, it is Holy Spirit at work to point out these things...because He wants us to experience the wholeness and freedom that He desires for us.

At the crack of dawn, while the sun is barely peeking over the horizon, you can stand in a dark room and barely make out the big things in the room: the sofa...the bed...the chair. However, as the sun breaks forth fully into day, you begin to see the smaller details: the book that's out of place...the spider web in the corner of the window...the layer of dust on your dresser.

The Lord does not show us everything at once. As we allow in more light from Holy Spirit, we will be shown those things He is pointing His finger at, illuminating the bruises one by one. The Lord is a gentleman...He never forces us to do anything. He points the way. The decision to act is ours alone. If He is showing you evidence of a bruise, you have a choice to ignore the evidence and "just live with it," or ask Him to reveal its core so that you can excise it. Excision is an act of your <u>will</u>.

These first two prayers in the Appendix are meant to help guide you if the Lord has shown you something, and you want to renounce it. Excision doesn't have to be a long process...merely a biblical one. The Lord desires your wholeness. He loves you so much that He wants you to experience the fullness of health in your body, in your soul and in your spirit.

There is one final prayer in the Appendix section that I also encourage you to pray: "A Declaration of Independence For Self" written by Pastor Sandy Mathis. In her vast experience counseling men and women in inner healing and deliverance (most of whom are in full-time ministry), her number one observation is that the overwhelming majority struggle with whether God truly loves them. She recently explained, "Most people would say they believe God loves other people, but when I ask them, 'Do you believe God loves YOU with all His heart?' invariably they admit they struggle with that."

We all struggle with accepting that we are special to the Father...that He adores us. Thus, this "Declaration of Independence for Self" is an important affirmation we should make...out loud, and often.

In the next chapter, I will share with you the essence of inner healing as the Lord has taught me over the years. Our ministry assignment is to help our wounded sisters loose themselves from all defiling spirits and appropriate the cleansing that the blood of Jesus provides. Then, He takes us by the hand and leads us into wholeness.

LETTER 16
The Call To Heal The Levitical Women

Dear Aleeyah,

This chapter has been particularly difficult to write. As memories of old wounds began surfacing, I knew I had to share a very personal part of the levitical journey: *inner healing*. This is a topic that is rarely discussed from the pulpit. As with most life lessons, my lesson in healing has spanned many years. In 1972, while part of the Music Ministry for Campus Crusade for Christ, I was asked to develop a one-woman show for secular women's colleges in the East. This was at the height of the Feminist Movement...and marketing wunderkind that I thought I was, I cleverly branded myself as *"Candi: A Liberated Woman."*

I was a such a fledgling in the Lord. Looking back on the memory, I was no more "liberated" than a sardine in a can. Yes, I had Jesus...and if I had died then and there, I would have gone to heaven. But I was far from free.

It's been 40 years...a biblical generation...and I'm still being set free. The inciting incident ("screenwriter terminology") for this chapter was a month-long period of intense sobbing. I didn't really know what was going on, for I wasn't particularly sad or depressed...nothing traumatic had been going on...and yet I was tapped into an inexplicable sorrow that drove me to the Lord day after day asking, *"Father, what's going on?"*

My introspective nature tried to examine what was happening in the spiritual realm, figuring there might be some collective, unseen wind of sorrow. Insight began to come as two friends, independently of each other, said something profound. One heard the Lord say to her, *"You will do anything to keep from having feelings."* A second one confided, *"I know there is a wall somewhere that is keeping me from breakthrough. I can feel it there, but am powerless to remove it."* Walls. Boy, am I familiar with them.

The Call To Feel

Jesus was referred to as a *"man of sorrows, acquainted with grief."* (Isaiah 53:3) The Hebrew word for *sorrow* is *ka'ab*, which means "to feel pain." Jesus was the embodiment of one who feels pain. That was part of His assignment...His calling. He was called to take upon Himself, and carry, the full ability to feel pain. I can hardly wrap my mind around that statement. He purposely chose not to use any defense mechanisms to avoid feeling. He did not drink, overmedicate, overeat, tell jokes, stay in a continual frenzy of busyness, watch TV, or talk on the phone. No, He chose to <u>feel</u> every bit of betrayal, snide remarks, beatings, torments of impending death...and He chose to feel what those He ministered to felt. In fact, I would wager that His uberdose of feelings gave Him direct insight into what demon was tormenting someone. With such knowledge, He could thereby call its name and cast it out.

Some months ago, I began having communion every day...just the Lord and me. That very act is saying, *"Lord, I am willing to drink Your cup. Whatever You had to go through, I'm here to partake of it, and share this with You."* Well, hello...if He is <u>the</u> *"man of sorrows,"* I should not be surprised to be feeling it too. But what does that mean?

Needed: Emotional Reconstruction Surgery

I am uncovering an insidious plot by the enemy. In this hour of increased wickedness, we need to be even more diligent to maintain a sensitive spirit – one that can <u>feel</u> the pain of others and deliver them. The ability to feel is truly a woman's territory. That's where we shine! But I want to submit to you, Aleeyah, that the enemy has thrown most of us into such a mass of hurts and childhood wounds that we have become too <u>scarred</u> to feel...too walled up to minister effectively.

If He is coming back soon and preparing a levitical people, He is not only purging us of defilements, but also gently inviting us to undergo emotional reconstruction surgery. When walls prevent us from feeling, they also prevent us from worshipping freely and feeling the outpouring of love the Father has to give...not only <u>to</u> us, but <u>through</u> us to others.

One Woman's Story

Barbara (not her real name) has walked with the Lord for many years. A strong woman of God, she heads up a well-known ministry. One night several years ago, I had a dream about this woman, and was surprised by the "dirty," sexual nature of this dream...for everything I knew about Barbara was her Christ-like walk with the Lord. The Lord began to reveal to me that early on in her life, she had been molested, and this early defilement was keeping her from all that God had for her. After much prayer, I called Barbara and asked if she would come for ministry.

On day 1, we tracked down that memory and she verbally renounced the perverse defiling spirit that had slimed her. She asked Jesus to set her free from it, and we thanked Him for the authority we have to cast out spirits in His name. Before going to bed, I asked the Lord for wisdom as to what to do next. That night, the Lord gave me a Word of Wisdom dream which has since become a cornerstone in understanding how we can be set free.

THE DREAM: "Free The Captives"
(January, 2003)

(As I wrote in my journal after awaking.)
I was with a group of young girls, between 3 and 10 years of age. It "seemed" they were all part of my family, and we were standing in front of a cage-like structure. Inside the cage were older females. There was a glass separation between us and them and I was trying to find a way to let them out or get us in. One particular older woman looked longingly at us, wanting to be reunited. She was old and wrinkled. It seemed it was my grandmother. The young ones were not in the cage. I was outside with them, and my desire was to reunite the old one with the young one. When the cage was opened, the older one came out and looked bewildered. But she reached out her hands for the young one and they embraced.

End of dream.

As I brought the dream before the Lord for His interpretation, I realized that He was telling me exactly what to do with Barbara: in Jesus' Name, call forth that little child and have Barbara embrace her fully into her life as an adult.

Here is what the Lord taught me as I recorded it in my journal:

"You saw in your dream the prison many people find themselves in. It wasn't the children who were imprisoned; it was the adults. I am teaching you a deep truth within the spiritual realm: just as My Father and Holy Spirit and I are one, so there is a triune unity within man. Many see it only as Body, Soul and Spirit...but there is also a triune unity within the soul itself, the seat of one's Mind, Will and Emotions. Many adults, like Barbara, because of the level of their wounding, have splintered off and disassociated from their "child" at the particular age of the wounding. There is a reason why I continued to welcome the children, because only when someone comes to me as a child can they see and feel and experience the wonder of My fullness. I said, 'Let the children come to me, and do not hinder them; for to such belongs the kingdom of heaven.'" (Matthew 19:13)

The Levitical Ministry Response

I took the wisdom the Lord showed me and applied it the next day. By an act of her will, I had Barbara:

- Identify with that wounded child part which had splintered off.

- Ask Jesus to come into her life, as that child.

- As the adult, invite that splintered off child to be integrated into her life, assuring Little Barbara that she would never be alone again...that she (the adult) would always be there with her and that Jesus was living inside and promised never to leave.

I then laid hands on her and prayed that the youth, wonder and vitality of that little child would freely course throughout her veins and restore her to the fullness of health and joy that the Father intended her to have. This is a revelation of inner healing and redemption I'm only beginning to understand. What I see is that the Father either allows or has designed the disassociation phenomenon in order to protect the core person (in this case, the Adult Barbara) and encapsulate the wounded Little Barbara until the time when she can be set free and full redemption and restoration takes place within the core adult personality.

As an aside, Barbara later told me that before coming to me for ministry, she walked down her stairs and looked at the photo of herself when she was 10 years old. A woman not normally given to emotions, she burst into tears. Regardless of whether she realized it or not, she was grieving the loss of this "little girl." I see this as Holy Spirit preparing her for what was about to take place.

Aleeyah, I submit to you for prayer and consideration that this redemptive process is one of the key ministry stewardships entrusted to the levitical woman, for it is vitally connected to the Father's heart.

As Isaiah 61:1 says, the Father anoints us for this very purpose:
- To bind up the *wounds* [i.e., splintered pieces] of the brokenhearted.
- To *proclaim* liberty [i.e., declare] to the *captives*.
- To open the door of the *prison* [i.e., the cage].
- To set the *captives* free.

You will be interested to learn the meaning of key Hebrew words in the Isaiah passage.
- *Liberty* is *derowr*, and it means "to move with total freedom and spontaneity of outflow." [i.e., creativity]
- *Captive* means something or someone "exiled, captured, or collected." The root of the word is *shebun* and carries the idea of subdivision into flashes or streams, such as a flame is split into different tongues or sparks.
- *Prison* is *peqach-gowach*. It is a "re-doubled" dungeon; also the opening of senses, especially the eyes.

I hope you are able to see the depth of wisdom that lies within the original Hebrew language. There are parts of us that were <u>subdivided</u> during severe wounding...captured... and thrown into a double-thick dungeon. Who else but the enemy of our souls has the desire, motivation and power to do that? But...when we release a captive – by reuniting the Adult core person with that Little Child that was driven into captivity – we set into motion an outflow of spontaneous freedom and creativity that begins to fully manifest in the person's life.

Have you observed people who look older than their years...compared with others the same age who are vibrant and alive and purposeful? I certainly have. This marvelous truth of reuniting the Adult and Wounded Child is redemption in action...it is precious to the Father.

The Good Shepherd

I was meditating on Matthew 18 and the role of the Shepherd in *"saving what was lost."* My mental picture is a little lamb off by itself, shivering in the cold as night hangs as a spectre overhead. Its heart-wrenching bleats echo into a cavernous loneliness I understand all too well. It is this "lost sheep" the Shepherd risks everything to save. Visualizing this lost lamb makes the inner healing journey come alive with new meaning.

The word *lost* is *apollumi* in the Greek. *Apo* means *off* in the sense of "being away from something it used to be near to." The base *ollumi* is a prolonged form of "to destroy, ruin or death." In Barbara's case, that little girl was lost, but now is fully integrated into her being...as God intended. Over time, Barbara has become more vibrant, as a woman, than she used to be. All praise belongs to the Good Shepherd whose heart is ever in search of the "lost lamb." That same Shepherd used a fledgling Levite and gave me "ears to hear" the word of wisdom shown to me in the January, 2003 dream.

The Father will <u>always</u> give us answers and solutions for the people to whom we are to minister. The answers may come in the form of dreams or visions which are part of the divine, metaphorical language of Pictures that the Lord loves to use.

He is pleased when we *"take heed to what we hear"* (Mark 4:24) and press in for further revelation. *"It is the glory of God to conceal things...but the glory of kings is to search things out."* (Proverbs 25:2) *"If you seek it like silver and search for it as for hidden treasures, then you will understand the fear of the Lord and find the knowledge of God. For the Lord gives wisdom; from his mouth come knowledge and understanding; he stores up sound wisdom for the upright..."* (Proverbs 2:3-7a)

How Do You Know When There Is A Lost Child - In You Or In Others?

I have found in my own life and in ministering to others that there are always clues that something within a person is missing. It calls out to us in varying ways. For some, it may be nightmares. For others, it may be a set of circumstances that keep coming up in your life over and over again. Take triangulation, for example. If you find yourself in a situation (work, social life, etc.) with two other people...and time and time again you are the one that gets hurt...you are the one who is betrayed, chances are there is an archaic root...and you will find a little child who was deeply wounded in the process.

My rule of thumb is two-fold:

1. If the behavior that manifests (anger, uncontrollable tears, anxiety, inappropriate actions) is so pronounced that it is keeping you from living the kind of life you know the Lord would want for you, that "woundedness" is crying out for attention. In essence, you are hearing that little lamb bleating, trying to get someone's attention...to track it down...and ultimately rescue it.

2. Commit to chase down the woundedness. I have had to do this in my own life many times over 40 years. The freedom I have in my inner life - well, it's not perfect, you understand...but the freedom I now enjoy is light years from when I began the journey. Bottom line: I have worked hard for it. I have cried, pushed through, been vulnerable to therapists, deliverance ministers and close friends. Generally, we are not able to go through our own inner healing alone. If you find yourself hearing the wounded bleats of a "little one" within you, I pray that you will ask God to show you who you can trust to bring about the Shepherd's healing for you. Your very life depends on it...and oh, what joy awaits!

As you become more free, you will easily spot the signs in others...and your levitical antennas and skills for healing and deliverance will develop. At that point, get ready. The Lord will use you to free others. It is His investment of ministry skills within you...He always takes inventory of who truly is about His business, and rejoices when we are found faithful.

A Personal Story

After being abandoned by my first husband, the Lord reunited me with my first love. Mike and I had gone separate ways for 30 years or so...and he had been deeply wounded by his divorce. It took several years for us to heal individually before we could marry and try to blend our families. We found joy in each other...but frankly, we struggled in the blending....so much so that we resorted to living apart when our sons were in their teen years. We came to the realization that our love, though strong, had to take second place to the commitment and stewardship we felt for our respective children.

It was during this "living separately" that I was deeply engaged in my own inner healing. I regularly met with a Christian therapist who was gifted in reconciling the adult core of who I was with deep wounds suffered as a child. This picture shows what was happening. This is a picture of me as an adult...but the old photo taken around the age of 3 really tells the story.

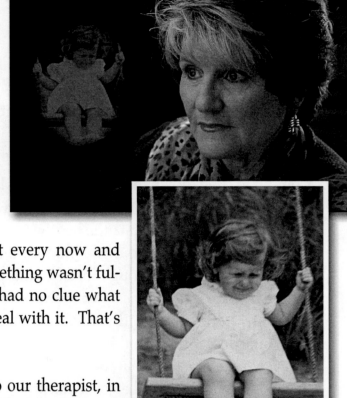

You see the child's sorrow clearly. In the top photo: though I appeared "together" on the outside, there was always an insecurity that went back that far. My Little Child (though un-identified at that time) would manifest every now and then. I "knew" instinctively that something wasn't fully right or whole deep inside...but I had no clue what was happening, much less how to deal with it. That's when I committed to seek help.

In September, 1998, I wrote to our therapist, in preparation for a consultation Mike had set up with her...to deal with his own inner healing issue.

My Letter To The Therapist:

"Mike said some significant things during our last weekend together I thought you would want to know. He said that during this time of living separately, he sees me as *thriving*...and him as *dying*. He remarked what a big change he's seen in me. Part of him is happy for me...the other part resentful that he's not experiencing the same. I said, '*Honey, the change you see is that during this separation, I've had the time and energy to face a lot of things within myself I wasn't at peace with. I've confronted a lot of my deepest 'fears' and am at peace with my Little Girl. I have come to embrace her.*' When I suggested that perhaps one reason for his depression is that he is not at peace with his Little Boy, he said emphatically, '*I don't want to make peace with my Little Boy...I want him dead!'* I said, *'No wonder you are depressed! He is fighting to live and you're trying to destroy a very vital part of yourself.'* When I reminded him of your description of the 3 parts of us: Adult, Child and Critical Parent, he added, *'There is no Adult here...and I want the Child dead.'"*

Mike died one month and 5 days later. No pain...his heart simply stopped.

I share this intimate story because it illustrates how vital it is to be at peace with the wounded child within us. It really is a matter of life and death. I believe that the Father, in His mercy, removed Mike from his torment of life. Remember, every day the Lord gives us a choice: *"I call heaven and earth to bear witness against you this day, that I have set before you life and death, blessings and cursings; therefore choose life, that both you and your descendants may live."* (Deuteronomy 30:19)

Memories Of Childhood Trauma May Surface Years Later

Just recently I was ministering to a woman who was extremely depressed and suicidal. I met with her to locate the open door to this present trauma. She was desperate to feel the presence of God again...for she found herself totally unable to feel. Toward the end of our time together, she burst into tears and confessed that when she was 5, the doctor told her mother that her young daughter had genital herpes. Her mother minimized it back then, telling her it was nothing...that she got it from a toilet seat. She then put medicine on it for minor cuts and bruises and sent her back off to school. The young girl grew up carrying around a sense of shame she should never have had to carry. The Lord eventually revealed in our present time of ministry that this was the incident where the enemy got access and began to mess with her thoughts and distort her view of herself. I finally said, as gently as I knew how, "You do know that you can't get genital herpes from a toilet seat, don't you? (pause) You were sexually abused. Do you have any memory of that?" She did not. It was not time to press her for memories. What the Lord meant to surface finally did...the rest will come in its time.

I have another close friend for whom a similar memory surfaced, much later in life, way past her 50's. She explained that she had sensed something wrong for years but didn't really know what it was. Her pastor said, "Pray about it. Ask God to show you the memory." That night, she asked the Lord to show her, and woke up having a dream about being in bed with her father. Terribly distraught, she stayed up all night trying to put the pieces of her life together. She had no memory of any such incident at all, though admitted having negative feelings toward her father most of her life. Her conflictedness about him now held new meaning.

Her pastor and I led this middle age woman to reconnect with that "lost little child" and she began the process of healing. About a month later she ran across part of an old journal she had written years before describing a dream wherein she, as an adult, watched a man "attack" a child about 3 or 4 years old who was taking a nap. The man hit the little girl over the head and broke her right hand. She wrote in her journal, "When I watched this child get attacked in the dream, I had no feelings at all for her." We helped her to see that the child was her...and explained that she had dissociated from the memory. In His graciousness, the Lord separated her from those memories because she was not yet ready to deal with them. But now, He allowed her to see when the molestation happened and to finally integrate that Little One fully into her life. This woman of God now displays an inner strength and resoluteness of wholeness she never had before. God is using her to heal many other women.

I share these two stories simply to show you that memory losses, especially of traumatic events, are very common. As ministers, we are learning more every day how gracious God is in the way He psychologically and emotionally protects us from hurts that we may not yet be ready to handle. He knows when the time is right to find and restore to wholeness another "lost lamb."

We should expect to see more and more women need this form of inner healing as we near the coming of the Lord. He is calling His levitical women. Within that calling is the need for cleansing from every defilement, even those defilements we have no memory of. That is the Father's heart.

Your Personal Call To Wholeness

Aleeyah, this chapter is all about an insidious plot by the enemy to get us so distracted by life that we never get around to become clean...and whole. If the Light the Father put in us is splintered into tongues of flames, or sparks....we will not shine as brightly as He intended in this ever-darkening world.

I urge you...and your daughters: be willing to pursue your own healing. It begins with your will. The Father desires our wholeness. As women, we were given an extra measure of <u>capacity</u> to feel the hurts of humanity. But there is a choice we must make every day, as we come into communion with Jesus. Will we drink His cup? Will we submit to take into our body the ability He had to *feel* those hurts? ***True levitical ministry as a woman begins inside your own heart.***

If you hear a lonely bleat somewhere deep inside of you, please know that the Shepherd is seeking out that which was lost. He is here with you.

SUGGESTED PRAYER:
Father, I lay myself open before You, for You are the only One I can truly trust. You are my Shepherd...and I need to open myself and allow You to redeem the shattered places in my heart. Please take away the hardness that has kept my feelings locked up. Take away the walls...the inability to feel...the shutting down when someone gets too close...the fear that overwhelms me when that tender, innocent Little Girl that is so much a part of me cries for attention. I'm afraid of her, Father, because I fear that if I ever just sit down and listen to her pain, I will be engulfed by waves of emotion that I've pushed down inside of me for a long, long time. This is not Your way, Lord. The burden is too heavy, and You said Your burden is light. I want to be at peace with that Little Girl. I want her to know You as I do and be reunited with the parts of me that have scattered, some that I don't even have memory of. I desire more than anything to be the complete and whole woman You created me to be.

[Speak to that Little Girl part of you]

Little One, I am here for you. I will never leave you. No one listened to you when you were so wounded...but I am listening. You are not alone. Tell me what you're feeling. [Be quiet and let her tell you. Write it down.] *Let's give ourselves to Jesus together and trust Him to bring about healing in the deepest part of our woundedness. He said that by coming to Him as a child we can enter the Kingdom of Heaven. I need you to help me do that. Lord, thank You that I can come to You as I am...and that You promised to redeem my soul. In Jesus' name, I submit my heart to You for healing. Amen."*

To Conclude This Chapter

I encourage you, Aleeyah, to take a break right now and just go sit in the Lord's presence. Be still...and know that He is God. He wants to bring that wounded Little Girl and the wonderful woman you are becoming into wholeness and healing. To Him, that is a most holy place...for that is where your heart is knitted together with His.

LETTER 17
Wisdom For The Journey

Dear Aleeyah,

In this chapter, I'd like to address a number of questions and issues that I have received over the years from women looking for God's wisdom and perspective in this evil day, especially regarding marriage and raising godly children. I will try to address them to you, not assuming that you are suffering in the particular situation, but simply to personalize my responses to the women you are seeking to help.

> *Q:*   *My husband and I are on two different levels regarding spiritual growth. I really want to serve the Lord, and he doesn't share my interest or sense of calling. What would the Lord have me do?*

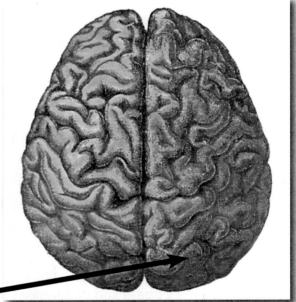

Cerebral Lobes. Source: Wikipedia (a derivative work of Gutenberg Encyclopedia). Author unknown. Image licensed by Creative Commons for public use.
http://commons.wikimedia.org/wiki/File: Cerebral_lobes.png.

A: This is an issue some women struggle with, for many are experiencing a strong *calling* to serve God. Women are, by nature, more attuned to spiritual things, because many are right-brain thinkers. It is how we are wired. In this diagram, you see there really is a right brain and a left one. Neither is inferior or superior, merely different. According to pioneering research of the brain by Ned Herrmann, founder of Hermann International, there is a section of the brain that is most sensitive to spiritual data: the lower area of the right hemisphere...found strong in many women. [64]

This area lies at the base of the skull, on top of the limbic system, where our feelings are based. God gave women the wiring to hear from God easily and sense Him with every fiber of our beings. It's not that women are more spiritual than men. We simply have different wiring. Men, on the other hand, have leadership gifts that God gave them to instruct and lead their families.

God holds husbands responsible for leading the family as Christ leads the Church. He holds wives responsible for nurturing and helping guide the children as befits a true helpmate of her husband. If there is not harmony on this, much pain and suffering will result. For example, if you married someone outside of the will of God, or had children outside of marriage and there is a non-father in the picture, I can assure you the home will be an easy battleground where the enemy wreaks havoc…simply because the "family" is not as God intended with children being nurtured under a covenantal umbrella of protection between a husband and wife.

Q: *What should I do if our family is in turmoil?*

A: The first biblical principle would be to confess all areas of sin or disobedience that led to the problem in the first place. That might involve: hardness of heart regarding sexual purity…fornication or adultery which led to unwanted pregnancies…caring more about your emotional needs as a woman rather than the needs of the children…not taking time to properly instruct your children in the ways of the Lord…allowing an abusive man in the home…not providing a safe and nurturing environment for children to grow freely without fear…staying with an unhealthy relationship out of fear of being able to support your children on your own. After confession of those sins, the second biblical principle is to change your behavior and situation according to biblical wisdom.

For example, let's say a woman has children by different fathers, and is with a new man who has no emotional tie to her children. He may be abusive, but she is afraid to leave him because she needs the money he brings into the family's operating budget. To make this situation line up with the Word of God will require great sacrifice as well as emotional and financial hardship. First of all, there must be an inner conviction that she has not modeled holiness and obedience to God's Word in front of her children…instead, she has modeled "doing what is expedient" because of the need for money. God will not bless this family.

What He is looking for is a woman who says, *"Lord, I have messed up and jeopardized my children's wellbeing, and their understanding of the sanctity of Your Word and the need to follow Your ways. I confess my sins before You* [list them, name them specifically] *and ask You for the strength to help me truly repent and raise my children according to the fear and admonition of the Lord."*

The action steps to turning the situation around according to the Word of God would include making a sincere commitment to live a life of celibacy until which time a godly man is brought along whose walk matches hers and who desires to be her covenantal husband, and who has a God-given love for her children. It also involves complete reliance on the Lord to meet her financial needs...not just shuttle them off somewhere else [possibly unsafe] so she can work three jobs. That is not wisdom. I would advise living near other women in similar circumstances who are likewise committed to following the Lord...to become a support group and take turns helping out with each other's children.

In this day of predators and child molesters, a godly mother must keep a watchful eye on anyone [another woman's child, for example] who could harm her children. God will hold her responsible for those she has brought into their world.

One Couple's Experience

I have a close friend whose first husband left her for another woman, and she was raising her 4-year old son alone. Within a couple of years, a new man came into her life, one who loved her and the Lord, and had custody of his 6-year old son. They married, entering a covenantal relationship before God, and attempted to raise these boys in a God-fearing, blended family. Her office was in the home, so she was able to provide good parental supervision during the day.

As the boys got older, jealousies developed between them, especially within her stepson who felt she favored her son over him. Because she was home all the time, her internal beacon [remember the quadrants in the brain] alerted her to his behavioral patterns of lying, manipulation and deceit. The boy's father could not see this because he was at work all day and his son, of course, was on his best behavior when dad was home.

One day, the couple went out on a date. The boys were old enough to stay at home. When they returned home, the wife found her son locked in his bedroom, not even to eat dinner that she had prepared for them. She began to inquire what was going on, only to discover that he lived in fear of the older boy every time she was gone. He was too young and small to defend himself.

Other signs of childhood rebellion and disobedience began to manifest. When she tried to bring discipline to her stepson, he [now a teenager] glared down at her and cursed her, refusing to acknowledge her position in the home. When his father came home, he had to deal with his son's disobedience. The boy rebelled against him, and left, saying he would go live with his mother. That lasted about three weeks, and he returned home broken and emotionally wounded [due to longstanding discord with his biological mother]. He begged his stepmother to let him move back in. Now, she had a very tough decision to make. She agonized before the Lord, asking for wisdom.

She ended up saying to her husband,
"I love you, and am committed to you and to our marriage. But I cannot allow Jimmy [not his real name] *to move back here. My first commitment has to be for the safety of my son. I believe Jimmy needs help, and more of your attention. The only solution right now is for you and he to move to a place of your own. I will help you all I can...but you need to tend to his needs, and I need to tend to those of my son. You and I will still be married and spend time together...my love for you will not change. But our sons are suffering because of no fault of their own."*

This couple ended up making a tremendous financial and emotional sacrifice for their children's wellbeing. They felt, in the long run, that it was the right thing for them to do before God. The tensions in the home were immediately gone, and their time spent together as the boys grew up were happy ones.

How Ezra Dealt With Mixed Marriages

There is a very chilling section in Ezra 9 and 10 regarding what happened when God called the Jews that had been scattered to return and rebuild the Temple. The problem centered on the Jews [a large percentage were priests and Levites] who intermarried with the very people God commanded them to annihilate: the Canaanites, Hitties, Perizzites, Jebusites, Ammonites, Moabites, Egyptians and the Amorites. A good percentage of these people groups had been compromised in the purity of their bloodline by Nephilim, for these peoples were noted for being immoral, ungodly, tyrannical and perverse.

So, here they were with all these children of mixed blood…and God was asking them to rebuild the Temple and reinstitute godliness in their homes and in their society. The principle to notice is that when we have gone outside God's parameters, we must deal with the consequences. Those consequences can be extremely difficult and sacrificial. Such is the journey of a wayward heart that wants God more than anything and is willing to personally sacrifice to become a godly mother. God's ways are narrow…but the road of obedience is paved with blessing and favor to those to choose it.

Q: *How should I deal with rebellious children?*

A: The number one parental responsibility is to raise our children in the fear and admonition of the Lord. The Bible is very strong on the need for proper discipline [administered in love and not anger] and instruction in the ways of the Lord. The second parental mandate is to provide children with an environment where they can grow spiritually. Let's face it: the world is increasingly wicked. Moreover, there often comes a time when a child tests parental guidelines and rebels. What are parents to do?

One of my close friends is Glenda Anderson Leonard, the co-founder of the Paul Anderson Youth Home in Vidalia, Georgia. The late Olympic gold medalist Paul Anderson – known as "the strongest man in the world" – and his wife Glenda began the PAYH in 1961 as a Christian rehabilitation center for troubled 16 to 20-year old teenage boys. These are young men who otherwise would be in jail. They are given a choice: *"Go to jail, or go to the PAYH and submit to their program."*

It's a tough program…but it works. For 50 years now, the PAYH has been a model of re-parenting troubled boys using biblical principles. Their success rate is somewhere around 94%…meaning that 94% of the boys, once they have graduated from their program, do not return to their rebellious, unlawful behavior. Instead, they have become godly young men living productive lives. God has honored this ministry, because the staff loves Him and adheres to His Word. I personally have recommended two young men there and seen miracles of how God restored not only the young men, but their families as well. I highly recommend them as a resource. Their website contains many helpful resources for parents dealing with rebellious children.[65]

Do Not Sacrifice The Non-Rebellious Children

There is a deep sorrow that rests on a family when all the attention is poured out on the one child who is constantly in trouble. This should not be. The PAYH, for example, will not tolerate rebellion of any sort. For example, the young man may be required to do physical, "non-productive" labor – such as carry a stack of heavy bricks or logs one at a time from one side of the football field to the other. The staff member assigned to him oversees this punishment, and watches for signs of true brokenness, at which time he pulls him aside and instructs him in how God would have had him behave.

The young men know that if they refuse to submit to the rules, they will have to leave the program. They don't want that, because the only other option is jail! The on-campus school is a privilege to those who are obedient. It is not a given. If they do not behave, they do chores and manual labor while the rest of the young men go to school, and eventually graduate the program. The PAYH staff are committed believers who genuinely love these boys…and the boys' wrong behavior melts in the face of consistent love and godly discipline. Unconditional love and godly discipline are what children need most.

You might say, *"I don't have time to watch my son carry logs from one end of the yard to another!"* This is where churches could come in…where there could be a weekly "boot-camp" for disciplinary problems within church families, and the men take turns monitoring it. But it needs to be monitored…and it needs to be tough, not something a child would look forward to on a whole Saturday afternoon.

Character flaws are becoming more apparent in today's young people. Consistent behaviors such as lying, stealing, doing drugs, selling drugs, molesting or beating other children – should not be allowed in the home, under any circumstances. To allow a rebellious child to remain in the home is to sacrifice the other children. The biblical mandate is to set up very strict behavioral guidelines in the home. If a teen [for example] refuses to obey, he or she must leave the home if all else has failed. Every child needs to know the rules…be assured of his or her parents' love…and understand the consequences for disobedience.

Nurture Their Spirits With Prayer

The PAYH staff meets every morning before the boys wake up and prays for the needs of each young man. As parents, we need to spend a lot of time interceding for our children…

bringing their needs before the Father…asking Him to deal mercifully with them, and to give us strength as parents to set godly standards in the home and stick by them.

Sometimes You Have To Let Them Go

I'll never forget when my then 3-year old son and I took in a stray neighborhood dog that was ready to birth puppies in the dead of winter. I saw her shivering outside and had to do something. We made a bed for her in the guest room closet, and throughout the night watched her give birth to five puppies…each of which looked like different dogs in the neighborhood! When she finished delivering, Mangy [what we named this adorable little mutt] turned her whole body around and pulled four of the puppies to her nipples, but left one stray puppy behind her.

I noticed that little pup was turning blue. Feeling sorry for it, I picked it up and put it to one of Mangy's nipples. Rather than welcome the pup, Mangy pushed that little one away, turned her body around again and brought the other four puppies to her to nurse.

I didn't want a puppy to die on my watch, so I was frantically calling anyone I could think of at that hour of night to find out what to do. The consensus was: *"There is nothing you can do. A mother knows when a pup will not survive. She turns her back on it and lets nature take its course."* Whaaat????

That went against every bit of mothering instinct I have. However, now that I'm in my seventh decade of life, I see things a little differently. There comes a time when a mother must give life to those who desire to be obedient and follow the ways of the Lord…they long for life…their hearts are bent towards righteousness. Give the nipple to them – figuratively speaking, of course.

This is what God does with us. He graciously gives us opportunities to respond to the discipline He gives to bring about true repentance. (Hebrews 12:5-11) But if we consistently ignore His discipline, He removes His hedge of protection and turns us over to the spirits we have chosen to follow. The Old Testament is one story after another of His children's disobedience, and the enemies He brought into their lives to deal harshly with them in hopes they would repent and return to their Father's arms.

The Story of Josh

My former neighbors – committed Christians – had one son whom they adored. When Josh [not his real name] became a teenager, he went wild: drugs…petty thefts…sneaking out and partying with friends. He spent time in jail, and generally made life miserable for his parents. We were not particularly close as neighbors in the sense of knowing everything that was going on, so after some time, we realized we had not seen Josh around the neighborhood anymore.

One day I saw Josh's mom in the yard and went over to visit. We had been having some problems with one of our sons at the time, so I was seeking wisdom.

I asked, *"I know you had some problems with Josh. How did you deal with him?"*

She said, *"It was the hardest thing we've ever done, but we finally told him he wasn't welcome to live at home any longer. He's been gone now for over a year. We hear from him occasionally, but that's about it."*

I asked, *"What if he came to you now, knocked on your door and said, 'I've learned my lesson. I'm broke and don't have anywhere else to go. Can I come home?' What would you and your husband do?"*

Her reply was this: *"We went to therapists and Christian counselors seeking wisdom, and we realized we never set the boundaries for him. We consistently gave in. So, at this stage in life, if he were to ask to come back home, we'd say, 'We're sorry you are going through a hard time, but we have every confidence that you will know what to do.' We would offer advice where we could, but basically say, 'You made a choice long ago to leave our home. You won't be able to come back.'"*

I have learned over the years that parental love that allows disobedience and rebellious behavior to remain in the home negatively impacts other children. Moreover, such love is not true love. It is co-dependency. For that child to have any chance to grow up in the fear and admonition of the Lord, he or she has to learn there are consequences for rebellion. A good parent will enforce godly standards and seek godly friends as a support group to whom the parent is accountable. And of course, pray without ceasing!

Recall Jared's Story In Chapter 4

During Jared's watch as patriarch for the children of God, the majority of these children – hundreds of thousands of them – rebelled, left the holy mountain and went to live with the children of Cain. Jared prayed for them, admonished them with tears, and warned, *"Do not go down the mountain to live like the children of Cain. If you do, you will not be able to return."* [66]

This was a patriarchal prophetic statement. This was a time in history when the evil had so corrupted the earth that it was impossible to return again to righteousness. I believe with all my heart that we are living in the time of Jared, in the sixth millennium after Creation. The evil has multiplied to such a degree that once someone *"goes down and tastes of it,"* it is impossible for them to return to righteous living.

> *"It is impossible to restore again to repentance those who have once been enlightened who have tasted the heavenly gift, and have become partakers of the Holy Spirit, and have tasted the goodness of the word of God and the powers of the age to come, if they then commit apostasy, since they crucify the Son of God on their own account and hold him up to contempt."* (Hebrews 6:4)

Examine The Fruit In Your Children

Just as a DNA test reveals the paternity of a child, so external behavioral fruit reveals the child's true spiritual identity: *Is he or she a child of God? Or a child of the devil?* A child of God exhibits not necessarily a perfect life, but a life that shows an active conscience that knows right from wrong, and an overall desire to do the right thing. Many children are devoid of conscience. Their character is flawed. They look for ways to break the rules... manipulate people to get their own way...try to get something for nothing...take what isn't theirs...and say what needs to be said to get people off their backs.

Jesus said, *"You will know them by their fruit."* (Matthew 7:16) If the fruit is bad, the root is bad.

This is not a book on parenting skills, so I will not delve too deeply into this area. Rather, this book is to help you identify the godly remnant who came from the loins of Ham. God is purging all of humanity, separating the wheat from the tares, and letting those go who do not want to follow the Way. He is seeking His remnant…the ones who will be faithful and serve Him when He returns.

The Importance of Spiritual Breathing

I learned this spiritual discipline in the early 70's when I was an eager young staff member of Campus Crusade for Christ. I want to share it with you, because it has been such a foundational tool in my own spiritual growth. Our founder, Dr. Bill Bright, developed this analogy as a way to explain the basics of walking with the Lord.

To keep on living, we have to physically exhale the carbon dioxide [CO_2] and inhale the oxygen [H_2O]. If we do not do this, we will die. The same is true in our spiritual lives: we must exhale and inhale spiritually.

What do I mean? When we sin, the Holy Spirit's job is to convict us of that sin. We instinctively know that we've done something wrong. The guilt rises within us. That's a good sign that Holy Spirit is doing His job. It is our job to listen. We **exhale** when we repent, or breathe confession out of our mouths to God. We **inhale** by filling ourselves up again by asking Holy Spirit to take over the control of that part of our lives that is giving us problems. Then we walk on by faith. As you well know, Aleeyah, we exhale and inhale physically many times during any given day. The same is true for spiritual breathing. Such is the faith walk. It's very simple, really…but there are two additional guidelines to consider: one is a warning…the other a blessing.

#1 Warning:

If we keep doing what God has shown us is wrong, our consciences begin to harden. When we are not truly repentant, our spiritual ears begin to malfunction and we no longer hear Holy Spirit's promptings. What happens next is that God turns us over to that sin, and we become enslaved by it. *"An evil man seeks only rebellion, and a cruel messenger will be sent against him."* (Proverbs 17:11) In other words, if we do not respond to a light warning to repent, God will send harsher discipline ["cruel messenger"].

#2 Blessing:

God does not want us to walk in fear of doing something wrong. A wonderful verse to keep us on the journey is 1 John 3:21: *"If our hearts do not condemn us, we have confidence before God."* We are to keep walking out our lives as unto the Lord. If Holy Spirit does not convict us of anything, then just keep walking. God knows our hearts, and knows when His child sincerely desires to please Him. He will speak up loud and clear when we get off course…so if we're not hearing the conviction, we are to continue the journey in peace.

LETTER 18
Reflections After 43 Years With The Lord

Dear Aleeyah,

On April 1st, I celebrated my 43rd spiritual birthday. Since we never know how long we have on this earth, I want to take the opportunity and share some transformational truths I have learned in my journey with the Lord. We reach a certain age where it becomes a "mandate" to pass on to the next generation the spiritual disciplines learned over the years...for sadly, so few nowadays seem to care about the things of the Lord. I fear that percentage will lessen in the days ahead. The way is narrow, and few are those who find it.

My prophetic call began in 2002, so I am relatively young compared to respected prophetic voices such as John Paul Jackson, Dr. Bill Hamon, Cindy Jacobs, Bob Jones, John Sandford, and Chuck Pierce. I have been especially blessed to have two strong prophetic leaders as mentors: Elizabeth Hairston, Founder of The Apostolic-Prophetic Connection and Barbara Wentroble, Founder of International Breakthrough Ministries. Both saw my calling, and ordained & commissioned me in 2009.

Since then, the Lord has had me speak out on many issues. *The Levitical Calling* was a divine assignment to help prepare His levitical children for His coming. Though my introverted nature much prefers to be off in a cave contemplating the things I am shown, I had to realize that whatever revelation the Lord was giving me wasn't just for <u>me</u>. It was for <u>you</u>. I believe this is one of the reasons He led me to write this book: He is calling you to embrace your <u>own</u> prophetic calling and go forth and disciple others.

My Personal Discipline As A Seer

Allow me to share my prophetic training ground. I share it because it is a highly valued spiritual discipline I dare never take for granted. We are coming to a time when it will be more and more difficult to focus on the things of the Lord. Even now, the atmosphere is filled with so much spiritual "static" that the Lord's voice is not as clear as it once was. We have opened the doors to such powers of darkness that it takes everything we have to shut off outside distraction...and retreat into silence before the Father.

Please hear me. Do <u>not</u> ever take your times with the Lord for granted. There is coming a time when you will give anything to hear Him like you used to. Remember this picture of the Levites surrounding the Tabernacle? When there was defilement in the camp and the Levites did not guard the altar of the Lord well, His Presence could not and would not abide with them. As our churches become more defiled, especially within the levitical worshippers, His Presence will depart. It will be more difficult to hear Him.

Artist: D'Ann Medlin. Used by permission.

Since 2002, the Lord began to flood my mind with prophetic dreams. My greatest joy over recent years has been to teach Hebraic principles of dream interpretation...for I believe that when the days become darker, the Lord will still be communicating with His prophets through dreams and visions. It is biblical. Acts 2 is being fulfilled across the globe...but the majority have no clue what God is saying to them.

Over the years, I have developed a personal discipline that God has blessed in my life. If you are a dreamer, and you do not yet have your own discipline, I hope you will find this helpful.

In Mark 4:24, Jesus said, *"Take heed to what you hear; with what measure you measure it will be measured to you again and will increase, especially to them who hear. For to him who has will be given; and from him who has not, even that which he has will be taken away."* When we pay attention to our dreams, and apply their meaning in our lives, more are given. As God trusts us with those meant only for <u>us</u>, He extends His trust to "hearing" for others...then leaders...then nations. But the most important things God looks for are: Do you have an ear to hear? Will you be found faithful to act on what you have heard?

Hebraic Dream Interpretation Principles

I have learned to distinguish a prophetic dream from fleshly ones...and with those that come from the Lord, I follow these steps which are beautifully shown us in Genesis 41:

- I write the dream down and come before the Lord with it.

- I ask the Holy Spirit to show me insights regarding the visual symbols He  points out and write down those things that come to mind. Most times I find biblical research is required. For instance, in one dream, I was with a group of people and all of a sudden spoke out for all to hear: *"I am a <u>YOD</u>!"* When I woke up, I asked, *"What in the world is a yod?"* Thus took me into a Hebrew lesson, and the significance of this particular letter of the alphabet, and why the Lord would have me identify with it so profoundly. (Note: The yod is part of this logo I designed for a new enterprise. It symbolizes the creative breath that is the core of the divine DNA given to us.)

- I follow the exact way that Joseph interpreted Pharoah's dream. He interpreted the metaphorical meaning of the symbols in Pharoah's dream...he prophesied to Pharoah based on what God showed him...and then exhorted him to apply what he was being told and store up food for 7 years in preparation for the famine that would follow.

- I date each dream, give it a title, and categorize it as to its purpose (call to intercession, prophetic direction, warning, word of knowledge, etc.).

- I file dreams by the year...so on January 1, I begin to review the previous year's dreams...to see if I am being obedient to what the Lord has shown me...and to seek clarification if there were some dreams I just didn't "get" at the time.

4 Stages To Go Through Before The Lord's Return

On April 1, I completed the final review of what the Lord showed me the year before. The findings were significant. I took the year's 60 dreams and looked at them by Seasons (1st Quarter, 2nd Quarter, etc.). What was particularly significant was that at the beginning of each subsequent quarter, the first title of the dream I received marked a shift in God's moving His children to another place. The <u>pattern</u> (i.e., big picture) began to unfold. It was exciting!

Dreams are very personal...and we often get so lost in *"What is God saying to me?"* that we ignore the fact that the message may <u>also</u> be for others. Aleeyah, I believe you have a prophetic calling, so please take heed to what I am saying: a large part of this calling is that many times, <u>you</u> are the message in a physical sense. Look at Ezekiel, Isaiah, Daniel, Zechariah. They saw dreams and visions...God called them as "mouthpieces" to speak out and declare what He was doing, because it impacted His children. What they were asked to go through was often <u>the</u> message to His people. This is still true today.

Here are the 4 stages I was shown leading up to the Lord's return. I ask you to bring them before the Lord and see if they resonate with what He has been showing you, and where you are now.

Stage #1 [Get Trained]

The Lord will lead you into a deeper training ground to hear His voice. Mentors will see your heart for the Lord and you will have access to them that you didn't have before. Never take for granted those leaders God puts in your life. He does not waste his valuable apostolic-prophetic leaders on just anyone.

If you see someone whose life of integrity and righteousness you respect, seek ways to learn from them. I have mentioned before that I always knew I was called to the Arts & Entertainment sector...but for 40 of those years, my "mission field" was to the secular. In the last decade, He has been shifting me to those within the church whom He is calling <u>out</u> of the pew, to be lights in the world.

When I first saw Elizabeth Hairston minister through dance, music, dramatic reading and singing, something resonated within me. I thought, *"Oh Lord, <u>this</u> is the way the gifts are to be used! Teach me!"* I was so hungry that I signed up to attend her conferences, even though I had no money at the time to do so. I invited her to dinner, and offered to drive her when she was in Atlanta. I knew I was in the presence of one whom the Lord entrusted with the proper handling of great giftedness. She walks in integrity, and holiness. I sought her out, and have served her for many years in whatever ways I can.

There was a stage wherein her life was in transition, and she was not accessible. One day I was given a personal invitation to attend a conference in Nashville, featuring Cindy Jacobs, Naomi Dowdy and Barbara Wentroble. Not coming from a charismatic, or prophetic background, I hadn't heard of any of them. But staring at the invitation, I <u>knew</u> I had to go...again, at personal financial expense. *(Key Lesson: You will never get anywhere without great personal and financial sacrifice!)*

At the conference, every time Barbara Wentroble spoke, I was in tears. I came home and shared this with a trusted friend. She said, *"God may be calling you to join her network."* He was indeed. I became an Executive Member of International Breakthrough Ministries, headquartered in Dallas. Barbara is an anointed prophet and apostolic leader who has a great anointing for breakthrough into the next level of service for the Lord. She also has a tremendous Marketplace thrust, and spoke to that part of my calling. She commissions leaders for breakthrough into the secular arenas to which they are called. There is an annual gathering for IbM members...for mentoring. She is available to those who are under her and who become financial partners of her ministry.

As you mature in your calling, God will call you to affiliate with ministries and leaders with whom you resonate. Examine their lives. Are they walking in integrity? Are they known for anointing <u>and</u> righteousness? When you do align, be prepared for financial sacrifice. As you seed into their ministries, God will seed into <u>you</u> what He has entrusted to <u>them</u>.

This first stage also involves an increase in anointing that you are entrusted to carry. You will grow in your personal giftedness and in embracing those gifts. All along this stage, God will be speaking to you in various ways (dreams, counsel from others, the Word, open & closed doors) to help you understand your specific calling. It will be unlike anyone else's, so don't get crazy trying to compare yourself with so-and-so. Your gifts are uniquely <u>you</u>. If you think you're too old for something, think again. This is <u>exactly</u> the time when you will receive this call. If you hear it, and push it away, agreeing with the negative thoughts, you will not get another chance. This is not a time when God is pleading with us to take an assignment. As He did with Isaiah, He spoke His mind and simply said, *"Who will go for us?"* (Isaiah 6) If Isaiah had not heeded the call and responded, do you actually think God would be pleading with him? No...He would quit speaking in his direction and move on to someone else *"who has ears to hear."*

Stage #2 [Articulate Your Message]

You will become acutely aware that the time is short. You will get your affairs in order, to prepare others for the financial crisis ahead. Some of you will hear the call to travel internationally. There is much spiritual hunger in the world. I have seen it. We have grown "fat" in this country...and God's heart is to take foundational truths oversees. Thus, if you are sensing this call, you're right on target with a lot of us.

Your personal message will form. There may come opportunities for leadership in the secular arena where you are. This is a time of God calling people <u>out</u> of the church and <u>into</u> the world, to be a beacon of truth and light. It's tough out here...ruthless...there are few voices of righteousness. You need to be very careful whom you allow into your life. This is the time when toxic people come creeping in: "gatekeepers" who block you at every turn or throw cold water on your plans and dreams...parasites who pull on you and refuse to take responsibility for their lives. Some that you used to hang with will either be taken out of your life, or you will have to let them go.

This is a time of the "Great Falling Away." Some of your children will see their spouses go in a total opposite direction, and it will be excruciatingly painful to witness the division in their homes. God is separating the Levites from the "Church," calling people away from a "religious mindset" where the leaders are no longer walking in holiness and integrity. As an aside, the Lord would never lead a believer to initiate divorce without biblical grounds...nor would He want you to live in an abusive situation where there is danger to you and/or your children. He will also be removing people through premature death...many times to protect them from jeopardizing their salvation. Every work you are called to do for the Lord, Aleeyah, will undergo purging regarding ungodly people who may be involved with it. Let it happen. Let them go.

You will become more acutely aware of your spiritual gifts, and you will be tested to see how you will steward them. This is a season of choices, and these choices will be tough: such as, *"Should I keep on doing what I'm doing in church...or should I enroll in this school to prepare me for what's coming?"* These are tough choices...but each one must be weighed according to what God is calling you to do.

There was a season wherein I financed a weekly radio program called "Unlock Your Dream." I felt such a burden to help people understand what God was saying to them.

What I discovered was that for the most part, listeners wanted something like a "psychic hotline" - call in and get a quick meaning and get on with their lives. One listener had the audacity to call me and say a dream had shaken her out of deep sleep so hard she almost kicked her boyfriend out of the bed. I said, *"You're sleeping with your boyfriend, and you want to know what God is saying to you?!"* She was unwilling to make the hard choice: move out and live a life of holiness....<u>then</u> listen to what God is saying to her.

I knew it was time to leave the program. First of all, the majority did not want to make the personal sacrifices to hear. Secondly, the Lord was calling me into the Executive MBA program, which took literally everything I had (energy, time, money and mental stretching). You will progress on the spiritual journey...or fall...by the choices you make in Stage #2. The Lord teaches us in Proverbs to *"buy knowledge and instruction."* (Proverbs 4:7) God cannot and will not promote you into a sector within our culture if you have not been properly trained and educated in the know-how to do what you're called to do...with excellence.

Stage #3 [Say Farewell]

This is a time of saying farewell to others who will not accompany you on the narrow path. The days will darken and become much more wicked. I do not take life for granted. I have seen family members' lives snuffed out in a moment. I may not have another time to say what is really on my heart. We are not promised tomorrow...only <u>today</u>.

In this stage, God will give you a platform to share your legacy with your family and friends...much like what I am doing with you, Aleeyah. I am pouring out what I have learned over 43 years walking with the Lord. When your time comes, take it. You may not get another chance. You may do it in writing (like I do), or gather your family around you as our Jewish ancestors did. You will want to communicate your heart...your belief and commitment to the Lord...your warning about the dark days ahead...your blessing and prayers for them...and your final admonition to walk in the ways of the Lord for He is coming soon. I have recorded prophetic words and prayers for my son...laid hands on him and prayed for him. I have been shown things about him in the days ahead, and I war on his behalf because of what the Lord showed me.

This is a time to war for your seed...that they rise up as warriors in the end-time army. The Lord promises that our children and grandchildren will inherit the earth and be blessed. They will <u>not</u> be moved. We must stand on that promise and declare it in the face of the enemy.

Once you advance in your calling, you will encounter training exercises to make sure you know how to breathe spiritually when the real avalanche comes, where every foundation you have trusted is shifted and you see it all crumble. It will. It will happen soon, I believe...though I do not have an exact timetable. No one does but the Father. What He has shown me, however, is that when the cataclysm begins, it will accelerate quickly. Only those who have built on a sure foundation will survive.

There will be much trauma, loss of life, confusion, riots and chaos. It will not be pretty. I have seen it over the years. In the last two years, especially, the sense of how close we are was underscored. God's training ground for you is to learn how to <u>breathe</u>....how to take in His holiness amidst chaos. One of the training assignments for your children right now is this: Do they make time for Him now, when things are hectic? If they do not, chances are they may not be able to survive what is coming.

Please hear me, Aleeyah: *it is critical to pull away.* Shut off the phones...leave your cell phone elsewhere...turn off the TV and radio. Even if you have grown up around noise and chaos, this is a time like none other when you must develop the spiritual discipline of shutting off the world and sitting in His presence in silence...with nothing but paper and pen and the Bible. Get comfortable with being in a position to hear. You may experience rejection or ridicule from those closest to you, but the Lord will provide comfort.

As the darkness of the world increases, the Lord is calling for those sounds of chaos to be met by sounds waves and frequencies of **praise**. He will anoint your praise and worship like never before, and use you to help others. If you are a levitical worshipper, your anointing will increase and others will come to you as at no other time. You will be called to invest in those who are spiritually and physically impoverished. Yes, it will come with sacrifice... but the Lord desires to show you His sufficiency.

This is also a time when God will restore those things for which you labored and lost, and you will glorify the Lord in how He uses your areas of brokenness in the lives of others. You will see all those broken things restored...and your joy will be like no other time, for you had even lost hope that this was possible.

Expect the supernatural and the miraculous. You will be given spiritual children and new business ventures which will be showered with favor. Submit to the Lord's emotional reconstruction surgery that He may be calling you to undertake because he wants to completely break down those strongholds of rejection and self-doubt that have encamped around you long enough.

Stage #4 [Watch God Work]

The veil of blindness that has been over the Jewish people will lift. That means that the *"fullness of Gentiles"* will have come in, which the Apostle Paul discusses in Romans 9 - 11. There will follow a great revival among God's chosen people...as millions of Jews will call upon Yeshua.

Next will come the "hour of darkness" that we have been hearing so much about. If we are still here while this is going on, then we will prophesy in the storm. This will be followed by an "open heaven." The Lord will provide portals throughout the world that will be accessed through worship...this will happen following the cataclysm coming upon us. At this time those family members who have been asleep spiritually will suddenly awaken and seek the Lord as never before. They will come to their destined place, and the prayers that you have sown will finally bear fruit!

This season will involve a time of examination for worship leaders. Those who have fallen will be purged, for His way is narrow and only for those who remain righteous and uncompromised. The greatest anointing during this incredible time in history will be for those who did not change colors...whose walk matches their talk...who operate without guile...who bear their hearts openly to others for accountability.

You will be given a time to "solo" - but this solo period is a critical test to see if you will remain true before Him when the adulations of others come...for it will. People from all over the world will pull on those with the greatest anointing. Great care must be given to pull away and bare your heart before God, and before your accountability partners, to purge you of every self-aggrandizement. God's desire and His standard is for each worshipper – especially those given ministry responsibility to teach and lead others – to remain as pure as when you began. This is also a time of transition, when many leaders will "pass the torch" of their ministries to younger ones whom God is raising up.

During this stage, we will actually witness the marking by God of the 144,000. If we happen to be at the "Marriage of the Lamb" at the time of this sealing of the 144,000, then the Lord will show you this by the spirit. I saw my grandchild being so marked...and he or she is not yet even a thought in my son's mind!

Leaders so designated by the Father will be wired to a new frequency. You will hear the General of the End-Time Army like never before. There will be a power grid and international interconnectedness with the heavens, and angels will manifest to assist you. This connection to the "power grid" will be aligned with your ancestral destiny that was long ago intended by the Father...but which was stolen by the enemy. During this stage, every wrong done to your forefathers will be righted and every sacrifice of prayer you have made on your family's behalf will bear fruit. God will be at work redeeming your ancestral legacy...and you, your children and grandchildren will forever sever all ties with freemasonry, occultism, witchcraft, perversion. Every manner of defilement will be cleansed and all curses broken.

Where your intended inheritance has been held up, there will be a shift and it will come to you. It will be sudden...and everything stolen from you will be yours to steward. Seek wisdom and buy knowledge in the area of financial stewardship, for God is looking for stewards during this transference of wealth.

Your greatest danger will be temptations to engage in sexual immorality, for the pull there will be great. Strengthen yourself now, while it is still day. Take care to avoid distractions. Remember, Noah had one assignment: *Build An Ark*. It took everything he had. He took his assignment seriously, worked at it day in and day out...and always began each day with the Lord.

At the end, you will look back on your entire life and see the incredible crimson thread that has linked each stage...where every sorrow finally reveals its divine purpose. You will see the panorama of your life and what it all meant, and how many lives you touched. Your heart will overflow with praise for the One who redeemed you and preserved you safely through every trial.

How special you are to the Lord.

LETTER 19
The Gateway To Freedom

Dear Aleeyah,

In this book, my deepest desire has been to make our Jewish forefathers come alive for you and invite you to walk beside me through the gateway to freedom – to the only place where we can be reconciled to one another.

The Tent of Shem – The Place of Reconciliation

While in prayer about this book, the Lord reminded me of several things and showed me His heart concerning this final chapter. First of all, there was, historically in our ancestry over the years, much enmity between the descendants of Japheth (Whites) and the descendants of Ham (Blacks). Racial walls did not begin with the African slave trade. From the very beginning after the Flood, our ancestors were both guilty of trying to enslave the other at various times.

> The Father then took me to Ephesians 2:11-12, 14:
> *"Remember that at one time you Gentiles in the flesh* (Blacks and Whites)*...remember that you were at that time separated from Christ, alienated from the commonwealth of Israel, and strangers to the covenants of promise...For he is our peace, who has made us both one, and has broken down the middle wall of hostility...that he might create in himself one new man...and reconcile us both to God in one body through the cross, thereby bringing the hostility to an end."* [Emphasis mine]

Let's look at these words. *Alienated* is *apallotrioo* which means "to be estranged away, to become a non-participant." *Commonwealth* is *politeia* which refers to a "citizenship" or a "community." Our problem as Whites and Blacks was not that we didn't like or

---

trust each other and thereby chose to hold onto our "issues" and "perceptions." No! The issue was that **we were <u>both</u> estranged from the *commonwealth of Israel.*** Neither of us was capable of full participation in the covenant promises of Israel.

The *commonwealth of Israel* is, spiritually and metaphorically speaking, a "foreign territory" for which neither of us had a birth certificate or a passport to be able to visit. By being so estranged, we became *"strangers to the covenants of promise."* We had no idea what they were. They were not part of our cultural frame of reference.

What are those *covenants of promise?* Everything that God promised Abraham, our earthly father…every blessing spelled out in Deuteronomy 28-30. We were "strangers" to those blessings. There was no magic prayer we could say to get <u>there</u>. We didn't even know they existed. We needed something more. We needed that wall keeping us from this *commonwealth of Israel* to be broken down!

That's what Jesus did: <u>He broke down this wall</u>! He tore down – not with force but with his blood – the barbed wire fence that kept the immigrants (us) from entering the "land of promise!" The Greek word for *broken down* is *luo,* the same word for *loose* which we discussed in the chapter, *"The Keys of Binding and Loosing."*

My prayer is that you will see, Aleeyah, that this book is my humble attempt to tell you about this Tent of Reconciliation, and point the way there. I want you there with me. It was in this Tent where I repented for the sins of my fathers and aligned with my Jewish forefathers. It was here where I found peace and restoration. It was a place of cleansing in my inner being…where the favor of God and the blessings *"going out and coming in"* became assured. An actual blood transfusion took place there. And it will be here where the blood of Jesus will remove our "dividing wall of hostility."

Aleeyah, I believe that you and I have a joint assignment: to help our respective sisters to *loose* ourselves from this "dividing wall" and become "one new (wo)man!" You cannot reconcile yourselves as a people any more than I can. We need each other to complete this assignment.

Prayer of Reconciliation

Here is the prayer that I am praying right now, as I write. Nothing would make me happier than if you pray it with me.

> *"In the name of Jesus, I loose myself from the hostility and distrust of the [Black race] [White race], going all the way back through the generations to my forefather [Japheth] [Ham]. Lord, I loose myself from and obliterate into nothingness every false construct and hostile stronghold that I allowed to be formed in my inner spirit. I loose myself from every misconception, every blame, every injustice, every prejudice, every accusation, every fear that my ancestors had for my brothers and sisters who have a special place of leadership in this time in history. I loose myself from this hostility and every misconception I have had about my [brothers and sisters of color] [white brothers and sisters] in the name and authority of Jesus. I bind myself to this "one new man" you promise in Ephesians 2, and ask that my [sisters of color] [white sisters] will join me in this new place of citizenship known as the commonwealth of Israel. I thank You for the promise of divine favor that we share in the Tent of Shem. Together, as daughters of Abraham, we have the covering of our Jewish forefathers. I thank You that here, in the Tent of Shem, the descendants of Japheth and the descendants of Ham will find true reconciliation, peace, and unconditional love for one another by the blood of the Lord Jesus who gave Himself for us and longs to make us one. It is in His name that I pray. Amen."*

Noah's Prophecy Clarified

In Genesis 9, Noah spoke a troubling, far-reaching prophecy: *"Blessed by the Lord my God be Shem; and let Canaan be his slave. God enlarge Japheth, and let him dwell in the tents of Shem; and let Canaan be his slave."* (Genesis 9:26-27)

For centuries, this verse has been twisted in horrible ways against your people. It has been used by many of my race to make your children think all people of color were cursed into enslavement.

This is a lie. This is not what this verse is saying. Aleeyah, I deeply repent to the Father, and to you, for how many of my forefathers used this verse as a cruel whip against the people of color. Forgive us. How much pain this has caused you and your children. It is despicable, and it deeply grieves the Father's heart.

What Noah Was Saying

- He singled out the line of Shem as the one through which Messiah would come.
- He blessed Japheth and opened the door for him and his descendants to dwell peaceably in the tents of Shem, which was His covering of blessing.
- He cursed the line of Canaan, Ham's youngest child. Please note that He did **not** curse Ham! He cursed the line of Canaan, because prophetically, Noah knew that an open door to the Nephilim would come again and try to pollute the Messianic bloodline after the Flood, and he foretold here that the breach would come through the line of Canaan. As history confirms, Canaan became the father of the nations God instructed the Hebrews to wipe out completely. There were seven of them: the Canaanites, Hittites, Girgashites, Hivites, Jebusites, Perizzites and Amorites. Hear me, Aleeyah: the call to wipe them out was <u>not</u> because they were black and deserving of slavery! That has been the lie perpetuated by the enemy for generations! It was because Canaan's descendents would carry the Nephilim-tainted blood, tempt the children of God to intermarry and thereby destroy any chance for the Messiah to come. History confirms Noah's prophecy: the nations in whom there were giants <u>*after*</u> the flood all descended from Canaan.

Canaan represented 25% of Ham's progeny. It's the other 75% whom God is calling now! That's you, Aleeyah, and your children!

He would not have called me to write this book if He had no use for you in this final hour. I would not have dedicated these years in research unless I knew in the depth of my being that He is calling His chosen ones from *"beyond the rivers of Ethiopia to bring to Him their sacrifice of praise."* (Zephaniah 3:10)

The message He gave me for you is this:

> ***The gateway to your freedom is not found in the Tent of Ham.***
> ***It is found in the Tent of Shem...in Ariel!***

The Lord is extending His outstretched hand of blessing to you and your children. He loves you, and is calling you to your finest hour.

It has always been about a choice…the choice of the children of Ham to embrace their ancestral line and go it alone in their own strength….OR repent before God for the sins of the fathers and choose to dwell in the tents of Shem along with Japheth!

The Story Of Ruth Illustrates This Principle

Ruth was a Moabitess. Her entire family line [Moab] descended from the incestuous relationship between Lot and his daughters. To re-cap the story, after her husband's death, Ruth chose to follow her mother-in-law Naomi, saying, *"Where you will go I will go…your people shall be my people, and Your God my God."* (Ruth 1:16) She **chose** to *loose* herself from godless Moab and *bind* herself to the tent of Shem. The Lord led her to Naomi's kinsman Boaz, and from this marital union between Boaz and Ruth, the messianic line continued and was greatly blessed.

The remnant of Shem and the remnant of Japheth are waiting for you, my sister! We need you and the remnant of Ham in this hour. We cannot possibly go through the spiritual battle that is facing us without our brothers and sisters of color. We need the strength that in is you *because of* what you were called to endure. It is the Lord's prayer that we are **one** as Jesus, the Holy Spirit and the Father are One.

Noah had three sons. Three in one!

In the dream I shared with you at the beginning of this book, the Lord clearly spoke a word of wisdom by saying that **if** the custody agreement regarding your children [i.e., legal right of guardianship] were written "in Ariel," – that is, in the spirit of our Jewish forefathers – then angelic warriors, the hosts of heaven, would fight for you! The scriptures teach the same thing: By blessing the seed of Abraham [Shem], you will automatically partake of the Abrahamic covenant: *"Blessings shall come upon you and overtake you…blessed shall you be in the city, and blessed shall you be in the field."* (Deuteronomy 28:2-3)

Aleeyah, God placed you in my dream, and on my heart. I believe I heard what was on His. You are His beloved. You have had to endure four hundred years of enslavement and been scattered all over the world. But you have held fast to your faith in the God Most High. You are a people whose time has come. He is waiting to embrace you and release you to your foreordained destiny.

In the final day, Ezekiel describes those who will be living in Jerusalem with the Lord Jesus. It is the day when His tent is extended to cover <u>all</u> of His children.

> *"So you shall divide this land among you according to the tribes of Israel. You shall allot it as <u>an inheritance for yourselves and for the aliens who reside among you and have begotten children among you. They shall be to you as native-born sons of Israel;</u> with you they shall be allotted an inheritance among the tribes of Israel. In whatever tribe the alien resides, there you shall assign him his inheritance, says the Lord God."* (Ezekiel 47:21-23) [Emphasis mine]

This is an incredible promise for you and me. The word *aliens* means "sojourners," those of us who have pulled aside from our own road to dwell next to our brothers of Shem in their land. This is precisely what it means by choosing to *"dwell in the tent of Shem."* We – the remnant from Japheth and Ham – will literally be given our <u>own</u> inheritance in the land <u>alongside</u> Shem. We will all worship and serve the Lord together, as He purposed before the foundation of the world.

I Saw Your Mansion In A Dream

After this past Thanksgiving dinner was over and the people left, I lay down on the couch and dozed off. There were two scenes to the dream, and I knew they were given to be included in the book.

> <u>Scene 1:</u> I am in a small room. A black woman sits in a chair with her head down, and a black man is disabled in some way. He can't get up and down by himself. I have my eyes closed singing *"Amazing Grace"* while playing a tiny one-octave keyboard.
>
> <u>Scene 2:</u> I am being driven somewhere. The driver turns down an obscure street, and at the end of the street I see the most gorgeous white-columned mansion. I am surprised because I have never seen it before. I ask the driver to go real slow so I can read the sign to find out what the building is. Suddenly, I am transported inside the building and on the wall there is a plaque: *"Into The Whirlwind."*

Whirlwind is a word pregnant with biblical meaning. The Hebrew is *ce'arah*, which means "to be tossed or sorely troubled." A whirlwind is an act of God. He took Elijah by a whirlwind…He answered Job out of a whirlwind…He takes princes and nations away with a whirlwind…He scatters the enemies of Israel by whirlwinds…those who sow the wind will reap a whirlwind. *"His way is in whirlwind and storm, and the clouds are the dust of his feet."* (Nahum 1:3)

Interpretation

- The instrument I am given to sing of God's amazing grace is tiny. The scene was far from pretentious. The instrument was nothing to write home about. There was no stage…I was not singing before a big audience. It was a small, humble home…yet I was allowed to see up close the suffering of your children. He sent me to communicate on a very personal one-on-one level the incredible love and grace He is extending to you and your children.

- He then let me see the mansion that I knew was yours. It was huge. It was beautiful. In dreams, buildings represent people's callings. The *mansion* was a testament to the calling He has for you. It was on an obscure street. It has been hidden, and reserved for you…and He has revealed it in its time.

- Once inside, as I stared at the plaque, the Lord spoke to my heart, *"My daughter, I am expanding your understanding of a people I drove away into the whirlwind. They have suffered and endured much, but I have prepared a remnant that is being called to their foreordained place in these Last Days. It is a high and noble calling. Theirs has been a long, hard road to get to this mansion. It has been hidden and tucked away….but now it is ready to be revealed. The plaque 'Into The Whirlwind' is a testament of the perseverance with which they have labored to cleanse their ancestral ground. This is the day I am returning the remnant of My children of color to their land of promise."*

The Custody Agreement

Aleeyah, what follows is the contractual agreement you asked my help in writing three years ago. It is written as a prayer, based on the prayers I believe you have prayed at the various sections. If you choose to dwell in the tent of Shem and walk in His ways, then He extends a wonderful promise. *"The blessed of the Lord shall inherit the earth…the righteous shall inherit the land, and dwell therein forever."* (Psalms 37:22, 29)

God bless you.

LETTER 20
Prayers Of Custodial Transference

Today, _____, [write date] a holy covenant is being ratified between you and the Lord.

Your Prayer of Release From Ancestral Sins and Strongholds

Holy Father, Righteous Judge who knows the sincerity of my prayer, I humble myself before You and honor You as my Savior, my Redeemer, my Heavenly Father, my Creator and my Lord. Blessed be Thy glorious name that is exalted above all blessing and praise. You are the Lord. You alone are worthy of my praise. I desire more than anything to walk before You in righteousness and holiness, and to raise my children in the fear and admonition of the Lord.

Father, Your Word teaches that when I confess the iniquity of my ancestors, and loose myself from every sin and treachery they committed against You…and if my heart is humbled before You, You promised to remember Your covenant with Abraham and heal my land.

Father, I acknowledge that salvation is from the Jews, and that through the generations You preserved the way of righteousness through the lines of Adam, Seth, Enosh, Cainan, Mahalalleel, Jared, Enoch, Methuselah, Lamech, Noah, Shem, and then to Abraham, Isaac and Jacob. Lord, I acknowledge that some of my ancestors sinned against You and rebelled against Your ways. They did not walk in humility and obedience. Some rose up against You and tried to destroy the messianic line…they murdered many children of Your people…they enslaved them and considered their lives as worthless. Father, I loose myself from their iniquity: from their rebellion, their worship of other gods, their giving over of their bodies to licentiousness. I loose myself from their hardness of heart toward You and indifference and cruelty to Your chosen people. I loose myself from the mindset of conquering and enslaving others…of taking pride in my own strength and independence…of seeking after forbidden knowledge and using it to control others.

Many years You strived with them and warned them; yet they would not give ear. Therefore You gave them into the hand of their enemies, and wiped out many kingdoms they built to honor their own strength. You are a holy and just God. Nevertheless, in Your great mercies You did not make an end of them, for Thou art gracious and merciful. You have a purpose for your children of color in these Last Days. Thank You, Lord, that You are a Redeemer and a Savior to all who come to You in humility and in truth. I desire to *"Dwell in the shelter of the Most High and abide in the shadow of the Almighty, and say to You, Lord, You are my refuge and my fortress; my God, in whom I trust."* (Psalms 91:1-2)

Father, I lay before You the orphan spirit that rested with Ham…who harbored within himself that he wasn't loved by You, or worthy of his father's blessing. I ask that You restore within me the blessing of my Heavenly Father, and I thank You that Your arm is outstretched with a desire to bless me.

I ask You to cleanse the bloodline that flows within me and transfuse me with the blood of the Lord Jesus, whose blood cleanses me of every iniquity, every sin, every transgression, as well as the door to curses that were opened by my forefathers' wickedness. Your Word says that the blood of Jesus *"redeemed us from the curse of the law, having become a curse for us…that in Christ Jesus the blessing of Abraham might come upon us, that we might receive the promise of the Spirit through faith."* (Galatians 3:13-14)

I choose, as an act of my will, to bind myself to the covenant You made with Abraham and I bless him and his children. I choose to dwell in the tent of Shem along with the remnant of Japheth. I choose to bind myself to the blessing of the Jewish people, to pray for the peace of Jerusalem, and to long for the day when the Lord Jesus will return and reign in the Holy Temple.

I present my body a living sacrifice, holy and acceptable to You…and ask that You enable me to live a life of holiness and obedience, and to raise my children in a way that pleases You and pass on to them how to walk in the ways of the Lord. I bind myself to the person You created me to be, and dedicate every gift to be used for Your glory…Yours alone. Use me, Father, to bring forth a pure praise in the earth…from beyond the rivers of Ethiopia. May I and my children be a blessing in the earth. Amen.

My Prayer For You

Holy Father, You have heard Aleeyah's prayer. You see the humility of heart and the burden she has for her children. I ask that from henceforth, You will honor Your promise to remove every *"sin of the fathers"* as far as the East is from the West. You promised in Your Word: *"Great peace have they which love thy law; nothing can make them stumble."* (Psalms 119:165)

Make her feet sure, Father. Let the blessings of Abraham overtake her in the cities and in the fields. I declare by faith that Aleeyah, and all her children who hereafter make this prayer their own, are free from every evil accusation. The enemy has no power over them to suppress them in poverty and enslave them in fleshly sins. No weapon formed against them will prosper…and every holy purpose for which they were created will be performed, by the power of Almighty God, Creator of the universe.

Aleeyah, since you have chosen to align yourself with the God of Israel and the promises He made to Abraham, Isaac and Jacob:

"May the Lord bless you and your children and keep you; the Lord make his face to shine upon you, and be gracious to you: The Lord lift up his countenance upon you, and give you peace." (Numbers 6:24-26)

APPENDIX A
Prayer Of Release From Freemasonry

This prayer of release from the curses of Freemasonry is taken from the book Masonry: Beyond the Light by Bill Schnoebelen and then appeared in the book Free From Freemasonry by Ron G. Campbell. This prayer can also be used if you know your family has been associated with the occult, witchcraft, sexual perversion, etc. Just be sure to name the "offense" as you pray.

"In the name of the Lord Jesus Christ, and by the authority I possess as a believer in Him, I declare that I am redeemed out of the hand of the devil. Through the blood of Jesus all my sins are forgiven. The blood of Jesus Christ, God's Son, is cleansing me right now from all sin. Through it I am righteous as if I have never sinned. Through the blood of Jesus I am sanctified, made holy, set apart for God and am a member of a chosen generation, a royal priesthood, holy nation, peculiar people, that I may show forth Your praises, Lord, who has called me out of darkness into Your marvelous light. My body is a temple of the Holy Spirit, redeemed and cleansed by the blood of Jesus. I belong to the Lord Jesus Christ, body, soul and spirit. His blood protects me from all evil.

In Jesus' name I confess right now that my ancestors have been guilty of idolatry. I call that sin, and I ask Jesus to completely remove that sin from my life and the life of my family. In the name of Jesus I rebuke any and all lying and deceitful spirits of Freemasonry that may think they still have a claim on my family or me. In Jesus' name I renounce the spirits of Freemasonry and declare that they no longer have power over me. For I am bought and paid for by the blood of Jesus shed on Calvary. I renounce any and all oaths made at the altar of Freemasonry, in Jesus' holy name.

By the power of His shed blood I also break any generational curses and bondage that may be oppressing me by oaths made by my parents or ancestors. And I nail all these things to the cross of Christ. I also break any and all power of the devil of any oaths over my children or grandchildren and command them to leave them alone. For they are under the blood of the Lamb of God. Because of the blood of Jesus, Satan has no more power over me or my family and no place in us. I renounce him and his host completely and declare them my enemies.

Jesus said these signs shall follow them that believe: In My name they shall cast out devils. I am a believer, and in the name of Jesus I exercise my authority and expel all evil spirits. I command them to leave me right now, according to the Word of God and in the name of Jesus. Forgetting those things which are behind, and reaching forth for the things which are before me, I press toward the mark for the prize of the high calling of God in Christ Jesus. Amen."[67]

APPENDIX B
A Prayer For Generational Cleansing
(Including Release From The Curse Of Illegitimacy)

"In the name of Jesus and by the power of His blood, I cancel all curses, all hexes and vexes all the way back to Adam and Eve that have been put upon me and my family.

I cancel every DNA memory that flows through me and my family that caused violence, meanness, sexual perversion, lewd thoughts, and demonic activity.

I ask forgiveness for everyone who caused illegitimacy in my family. I break the curse of illegitimacy over my family all the way back to Adam and Eve, which has resulted in hindrances to worship, prayer, and reading God's Word.

No longer will you, satan, kill, destroy and steal from me and my family because I stand in the gap and choose to have an enjoyable life and have it in abundance, to the full till it overflows with no lack.

I make this prayer in the powerful name of Jesus Christ. Amen."

APPENDIX C
A Declaration of Independence For Self

"I refuse to be insecure any longer because I am loved and highly favored of God.

I cancel all DNA thoughts of insecurity that flow through my body.

I confess that the eyes of my heart have been flooded with light and I know that God has blessed me with every spiritual blessing in Christ. God chose me. He picked me out for Himself. He foreordained me. He planned in love for me to be adopted as His own child. I pleased Him and I am His kind intent. I could never have been a mistake. I was created by God...not simply the result of a biological act between two people.

God has more thoughts of me than the grains of sand. God has more thoughts of me than any beach in this world. Father, You have more thoughts of me than all the glass and concrete in this world. I know that You favor and delight in me because You have my picture tattooed on each of your hands. I delight that You have compassion for me and could not forget me.

I choose to only speak life over myself from this moment forth. I crucify every godless thought of myself and only believe what Your Word says. I am loved and highly favored by You. You made me, Lord...and I am very good. I refuse to be insecure any more! I am blessed, happy and secure because my refuge is in You."

* All scripture taken from the Amplified Bible: Ephesians 1; Psalms 139:13-18; Jeremiah 33:22; Psalms 40:5; Psalms 41:11; 84:11; Leviticus 19:28; Isaiah 49:16; Genesis 1:31.

ENDNOTES

1 The Forgotten Books of Eden, *Second Book of Adam and Eve*, (World Bible Publishers, 1927), Chapter IX:5, pg. 67.

2 Ibid, Chapter X:3-4, pg. 67.

3 Ibid, Chapter XI, pgs. 67-68.

4 Ibid, Chapter XII:10, pg. 69.

5 Ibid.

6 Ken Johnson, Ancient Book of Jasher, (Biblefacts Ministries, www.biblefacts.org, 2008, Chapter 2:3-4, pg. 8.

7 Jasher, Chapter 2:11-14, pg. 9.

8 *The Second Book of Adam and Eve*, Chapter XVI:6-9, pg. 71.

10 *The Second Book of Adam and Eve,*, Chapter XVII:39-47, pgs. 74-75.

11 *The Second Book of Adam and Eve*, Chapter XX, pgs. 76-77.

12 *The Second Book of Adam and Eve*, Chapter XXI, pgs. 79-80.

13 Jasher, Chapter 3, pgs. 10-12.

14 Jasher, Chapter 3:17-20, pg. 11.

15 Jasher, Chapter 3:23-32, pg. 11.

16 The Forgotten Books of Eden, *Secrets of Enoch*, (World Bible Publishers, 1927), Chapters XXII and XXIII, pgs. 88-89.

17 *Secrets of Enoch*, Chapter XLIV, pg. 97.

18 *Secrets of Enoch*, Chapter XLVIII and Revelation 11.

19 Jasher, Chapter 4:17-18, pgs. 12-13.

20 Lost Book of Enoch, A Comprehensive Transliteration by Joseph B. Lumpkin, (Blountsville, AL: Fifth Estate Publishers, 2004), Chapter 6, pgs. 5-6.

21 "Falashas: The Forgotten Jews," *Baltimore Jewish Times*, November 9, 1979.

22 www.jewishvirtuallibrary.org/jsource/Judaism/ejhist.html.

23 www.weeklyworldnews.com/headlines/9322/ark-of-the-covenant-revealed/.

24 The Holy Bible, Today's New International Version, © 2005, Zondervan.

25 Jasher, Chapters 11 and 12, pgs. 23-29.

26 Jasher, Chapter 24, pgs. 51-53.

27 Jasher, Chapter 26:17, pg. 55.

28 Jasher, Chapter 26:28, pg. 56.

29 Jasher, Chapter 28:18, pg. 58.

30 Jasher, Chapter 29:9-11, pg. 59.

31 Lost Book of Enoch, Chapter 6, pgs. 5-6.

[32] <u>Lost Book of Enoch</u>, Chapter 7, pgs. 6-7.

[33] <u>Lost Book of Enoch</u>, Chapter 8, pg. 8.

[34] <u>Lost Book of Enoch</u>, Chapter 15, pgs. 21-23.

[35] www.bibleprobe.com/nephilim.htm.

[36] Randy DeMain, <u>The Nephilim Agenda</u>, (Maricopa, Arizona: XP Publishing, 2010), pgs. 165-167.

[37] Ibid.

[38] www.medicine.gu.se/english/phcm/occup_enviro/research/Sound_Environment_and_Health/soundcharacteristic_and_perception/low-frequency-noise-and-human-response/.

[39] <u>Lost Book of Enoch</u>, Chapter 10:11-12, pg. 13.

[40] *The Second Book of Adam and Eve*, Chapter XX:1-4, pgs. 76-77.

[41] *The Second Book of Adam and Eve*, Chapter XX:5-10, pg. 77.

[42] Ibid.

[43] www.100prozentgospel.de.

[44] Psalms 44: 9-17a, George Lamsa's translation of <u>The Holy Bible</u> from the Peshitta.

[45] Merrill F. Unger, <u>Unger's Bible Dictionary</u>, (Chicago, IL: Moody Bible Institute of Chicago, 1969), pg. 753.

[46] <u>Jasher</u>, Chapter 7:23, pg. 17.

[47] Joel A. Freeman and Don B. Griffin, <u>Return To Glory: The Powerful Stirring of the Black Race</u>, (Shippensburg, PA: Treasure House, 2003), pgs. 44-45.

48 Ibid, pg. 65. [Referring to Chancellor Williams, The Destruction of Black Civilization: Great Issues of a Race From 4500 B.C. to 2000 A.D. Chicago: Third World Press, 1987, pg. 303.]

49 Ibid, pg. 47.

50 Jasher, Chapter 7:46; 8:10-11, pgs. 18-19.

51 Jasher, Chapter 8:33-36, pg. 20.

52 DeMain, pg. 64.

53 Flavius Josephus, The New Complete Works of Josephus, (Grand Rapids, MI: Kregel Publications, 1999, Antiquities of the Jews, Book 1, Chapter 4:2, pg. 56.

54 E.W. Bullinger, The Companion Bible, Appendix 28, pg 29.

55 Drs. Christian and Robin Harfouche, Battles of the Elohim: They Walked As Men, (Shippensburg, PA: Destiny Image Publishers, Inc., 2011, pg. 3.

56 Jasher, Chapter 26:30-38, pg. 56.

57 Jasher, Chapter 72:22-24, pg. 150.

58 Jasher, Chapter 72:34-36, pg. 150.

59 Jasher, Chapter 73:2-3, pg. 151.

60 Jasher, Appendix B, pg. 189.

61 Ron G. Campbell, Free From Freemasonry, (Ventura, CA: Regal Books, 1999), pgs. 168-170.

62 www.bfwitness.org.

[63] James Strong, <u>Strong's Exhaustive Concordance</u>, (Nashville, TN: Crusade Bible Publishers, Inc.), Hebrew Dictionary, No. 4464, pg. 67.

[64] Herrmann International, www.hbdi.org.

[65] Paul Anderson Youth Home, Vidalia, GA, www.payh.org.

[66] *The Second Book of Adam and Eve,* Chapter XX, pg. 78.

[67] Bill Schnoebelen, <u>Masonry: Beyond The Light</u>, (Chino, CA: Chick Publications, 1991), pgs. 268-270, in Campbell, <u>Free From Freemasonry</u>, pgs. 186-187.

BIBLIOGRAPHY

Ariel, Rabbi Yisrael. The Odyssey of the Third Temple. Jerusalem, Israel: G. Israel Publications & Products, Ltd. and The Temple Institute, 5753 B.C.E.

Campbell, Ron G. Free From Freemasonry. Ventura, CA: Regal Books, 1999.

DeMain, Randy. The Nephilim Agenda. Maricopa, Arizona: XP Publishing, 2010.

The Forgotten Books of Eden. *Edited by Rutherford H. Platt, Jr.* Published by World Bible Publishers, Inc. Copyright by Alpha House, Inc., 1927.

Freeman, Joel A. and Griffin, Don B. Return To Glory: *The Powerful Stirring of the Black Race.* Shippensburg, PA: Treasure House [an imprint of Destiny Image Publishers, Inc.], 2003.

Harfouche, Drs. Christian and Robin. Battles of the Elohim: *They Walked As Men.* Shippensburg, PA: Destiny Image Publishers, Inc., 2011.

Johnson, Ken, Th.D. Ancient Book of Jasher, A New Annotated Edition. Published by Biblefacts Ministries, www.Biblefacts.org, 2008.

Josephus, Flavius. The New Complete Works of Josephus. Grand Rapids, MI: Kregel Publications, 1999.

Long, Candace. The Levitical Calling. Roswell, GA: auDEO Publications, 2008.

The Lost Book of Enoch. *A Comprehensive Transliteration by Joseph B. Lumpkin.* Blountsville, AL: Fifth Estate Publishers, 2004.

<u>The Lost Books of the Bible</u>. *Translated From The Original Tongues.* Published by World Bible Publishers, Inc. Copyright by Alpha House, Inc., 1926.

Strong, James. <u>Strong's Exhaustive Concordance</u>. Nashville, TN: Crusade Bible Publishers, Inc.

Unger, Merrill F. <u>Unger's Bible Dictionary</u>. Chicago, IL: Moody Bible Institute of Chicago, 1969.

ABOUT THE AUTHOR

Candace Long, MBA

Candace Long is Founder of Creativity Training Institute, based in Atlanta, Georgia. She is also a 40-year Arts veteran: Writer, Composer, Producer, Arts Leader and Marketplace Minister. She is a biblical commentator on inspired creativity and helps others understand their unique callings.

She teaches business leaders how to discern "good ideas" from "God ideas," how to empower creatives to hear revelatory insight, and instructs them how to take an inspired idea all the way from conception to the marketplace. She is gifted in dream interpretation and teaches how God can use dreams to plant seeds of destiny and how we can unlock our own personal dreams using Hebraic interpretive methods.

A prolific writer, Candace has written six screenplays and is an award-winning songwriter and broadcast producer. In 2001, she produced the world premiere of her musical, *A Time To Dance*. When opening night was scheduled on the ill-fated September 11th, 2001, she was plunged into personal and financial devastation. In her subsequent three-year "wilderness," God taught her over sixty biblical principles on how to walk in one's giftedness and survive the creative journey. This journey is chronicled in the ground-breaking book, *Wired For Creativity*.

She has served as Vice-Chair of Women In Film & Television International, President of Women In Film & Television Atlanta, and was appointed by Gov. Roy Barnes to serve on the Georgia Film & Music Advisory Commission. Currently she is 2nd Vice-President of the National League of American Pen Women, the nation's oldest organization for creative women.

Candace committed her life to Jesus Christ in 1969 and served with Campus Crusade for Christ's Music Ministry until 1976. From the beginning, she knew she was called to the Arts & Entertainment sectors. In the early 70's, she toured college campuses as a one-woman show billed as "A Liberated Woman" at the height of the feminist movement. One of her personal mandates is to demonstrate a spirit of excellence in the stewardship of God-given gifts and inspire it in others.

Her tenure as a "creative" gives Candace unique insight into how the enemy uses music and the arts to spew defilement inside the Church and on those He is calling as Levites. Her book, *The Levitical Calling*, is a much-needed voice for the call to holiness, as the Lord prepares a people for His coming.

In 2009, she was ordained as a Prophet by Dr. Elizabeth Hairston-McBurrows, Founder of The Apostolic-Prophetic Connection and commissioned as a Marketplace Apostle by Dr. Barbara Wentroble, President and Founding Apostle of International Breakthrough Ministries in Dallas, Texas.

To contact the author for speaking engagements:

Candace Long
Founder/CEO
Creativity Training Institute
885 Woodstock Road
Suite 430 – 337
Roswell, GA 30075-8212
Toll-Free: 1 (866) 308-4850
candace@candacelong.com
www.CandaceLong.com

To order this book or other books & music by Candace Long: ***www.candacelong.com***